SHERLOCKED

The Official Escape Room
PUZZLE BOOK

A STUDIO PRESS BOOK

First published in the UK in 2020 by Studio Press,
an imprint of Bonnier Books UK,
The Plaza, 535 King's Road, London SW10 0SZ
Owned by Bonnier Books,
Sveavägen 56, Stockholm, Sweden

www.studiopressbooks.co.uk
www.bonnierbooks.co.uk

© Studio Press 2020

1 3 5 7 9 10 8 6 4 2

ISBN 978-17874-1-769-4

MIX
Paper from
responsible sources
FSC® C018072

Concept by Sophie Blackman
Written by Jason Edinger, Mike Kalyan and Tom Ue
Puzzles by Jason Edinger and Mike Kalyan
Edited by Sophie Blackman
Illustrated by James Newman Gray, Martin Bustamante and Nia Williams
Production by Emma Kidd
Designed by Nia Williams

A CIP catalogue for this book is available from the British Library
Printed and bound in the United Kingdom

SHERLOCKED

The Official Escape Room
PUZZLE BOOK

STUDIO
PRESS

ᛒRIEFING

D^{ear reader,}

Firstly, we must congratulate you on being drawn into such a
seemingly complex tome, for it shows a fortitude of intellect that
Holmes himself would admire. Within the pages of this book you
shall find a tale of multiple mysteries – and one with multiple
resolutions. However, please do heed the following words of
advice before you begin.

You will be asked a series of questions as the narrative
progresses, and it is down to you, reader, to solve these puzzles.
Some will invariably pose more difficulty to you than others.
Should you find any one of the puzzles a struggle, turn to pages
224 to 239, where you will find a series of hints. We advise you
to stop immediately upon reaching each question, and to answer
each in turn before proceeding further with the story.

You will find documents on pages 220 to 223 for your
perusal. Familiarise yourself with these and refer to them as the
need arises. You are likely have other resources at your disposal,
from reference books to more modern technological gadgets and
instruments. Please do make use of these on occasions when an
answer doesn't present itself to you with ease.

You would do well to keep a notebook or some sheets of
lined paper to hand, should you wish to jot down your musings
or observations regarding the characters, locations and timings

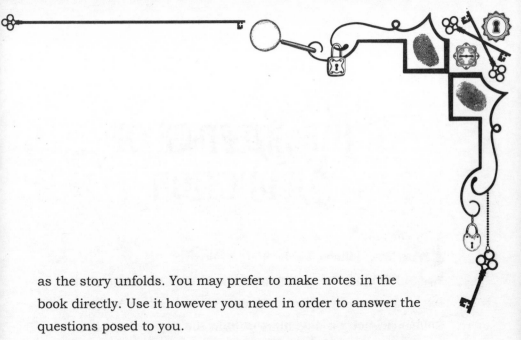

as the story unfolds. You may prefer to make notes in the book directly. Use it however you need in order to answer the questions posed to you.

The most valuable piece of advice we can give you is this: have your wits about you as you progress though this tale. This is no ordinary book. Clues to the puzzles – and therefore to the truth – can lie in any number of places. The smallest of details can attest to the accuracy of someone's words; the scratchings of a pencil can be viewed from more than one angle; and the cover of a book can hide answers in plain sight.

You are now ready to turn the page and begin. We wish you nothing but the best of luck on your journey through *Sherlocked!*

Arthur Conan Doyle.

THE
CONAN DOYLE ESTATE

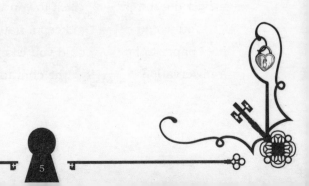

THE SCIENCE OF DEDUCTION

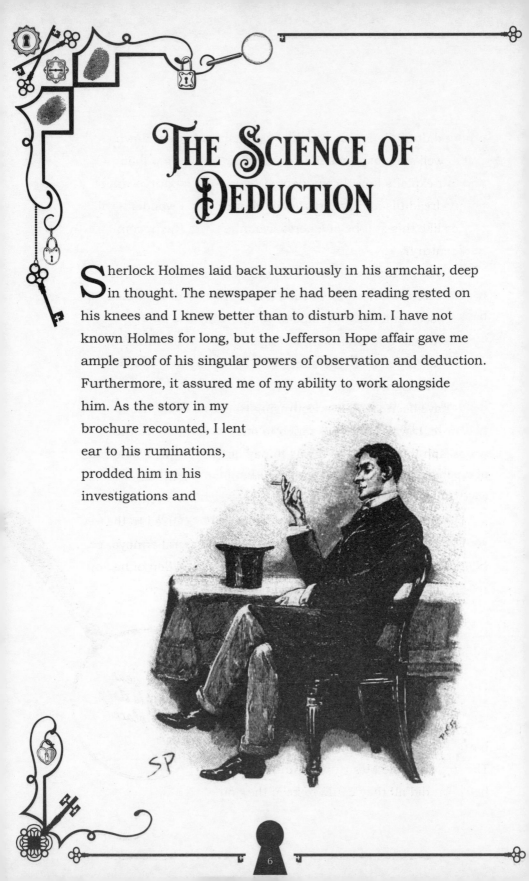

Sherlock Holmes laid back luxuriously in his armchair, deep in thought. The newspaper he had been reading rested on his knees and I knew better than to disturb him. I have not known Holmes for long, but the Jefferson Hope affair gave me ample proof of his singular powers of observation and deduction. Furthermore, it assured me of my ability to work alongside him. As the story in my brochure recounted, I lent ear to his ruminations, prodded him in his investigations and

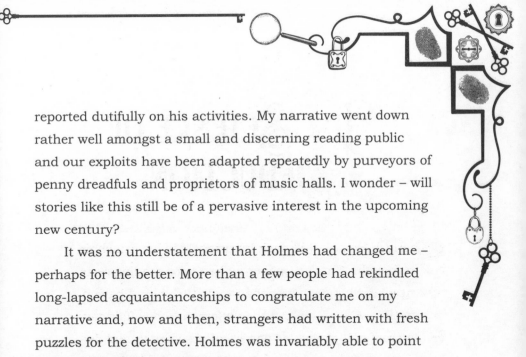

reported dutifully on his activities. My narrative went down rather well amongst a small and discerning reading public and our exploits have been adapted repeatedly by purveyors of penny dreadfuls and proprietors of music halls. I wonder – will stories like this still be of a pervasive interest in the upcoming new century?

It was no understatement that Holmes had changed me – perhaps for the better. More than a few people had rekindled long-lapsed acquaintanceships to congratulate me on my narrative and, now and then, strangers had written with fresh puzzles for the detective. Holmes was invariably able to point them in the right direction.

I have been steadily encouraging Holmes to read the brochure. It was written as much to offer a corrective to the paragraph in the *Echo* as it was to pay homage to the consulting detective and the practical applications of his remarkable gifts. I had given Holmes a copy when my batch arrived and I scattered a few around our Baker Street flat. I referred to the story whenever an opportunity arose. To my natural annoyance, he shared none of my enthusiasm, gave no suggestion of having read it and displayed no inclination of wishing to do so.

The date was 18 May; it was a beautiful Sunday morning following a week of incessant downpours.

For a whole seven days, the skies poured without inhibition and Londoners from every walk of life battled with banks of mud and water. The indefatigable Mrs Hudson and Lydia, her help, did all they could to keep the house

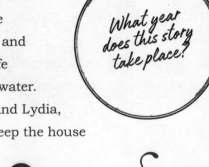

What year does this story take place?

clean, staring daggers at anyone who passed through the door. That morning, Mrs Hudson had opened the windows to air out our sitting room and the light made the polished surfaces glimmer. The irresistible sense of possibility in the air was heartening to me. I was a late riser, and shortly after 10 a.m., I had only just sat down to my toast and coffee when Holmes woke from his reverie and strode to my side.

"Good morning, my dear Watson," he said cheerily.

"Holmes," I answered.

"Have you any plans this morning?"

"I have some letters to write and the novel that I began last night." I conceded to myself that my projects pale in comparison to whatever Holmes may have in mind.

"Good," he said, "I have here a puzzle that will interest you, a follow-up, perhaps, to our little *Study in Scarlet*. You have been so good as to express interest in my work and to chronicle it for the encouragement of future youths. On this occasion, I may benefit from your counsel. And who knows? We may well find ourselves in a tight corner before the sun sets. The real world, with its curves and turns, is far stranger than that between covers. I'd go so far as to say: a couple of months spent studying the annals of crime would round out the professional's education more profitably than a library subscription."

Holmes handed me the paper he was meditating over. "Read it aloud," he entreated. "Perhaps hearing it will furnish us with fresh insights."

I poured myself some coffee, took a sip and read from the front page of the Sunday morning's *Daily Telegraph*:

DAILY TELEGRAPH

BURGLARY AT THE NATURAL HISTORY MUSEUM

A burglar has broken into the Natural History Museum. The event took place early Saturday evening, just after closing time at 6 p.m. During his round, Mr Miles Merton, one of the security guards on duty, noticed that that the glass in one of the windows had been smashed. Mr Merton's cries brought around a number of fellow guards, plus a junior constable patrolling the streets of Kensington.

A thorough examination of the mineralogy collection, the gallery in question, was conducted and it revealed the unconscious body of Mr Charles Wright, a guard who shares Mr Merton's watch. Mr Wright had suffered a blow but was otherwise unharmed. He could offer the investigators few details regarding the burglary. Mr Wright had been walking his round, much as he has been doing for the past four decades, when the sound of a whistle encouraged him to look behind him. He had scarcely done so when he was struck on the head, so he is unable to identify his attacker.

Officials remain baffled. Nothing appeared to have been stolen despite the inestimable historical and scientific value of the museum's collections. An inventory was conducted immediately, and all items accounted for. The new mineralogy exhibit in particular boasts one of the world's most extensive collections of rare and foreign gems and earth metals, many of which are on loan from foreign governments and private collectors.

Museum staff quickly cleared away the glass shards from the broken window in the interest of public safety and to avoid additional scratches to the museum's wooden floors. The window has been examined carefully. While it is sufficiently large to accommodate an adult, there are traces leading neither in nor out of it. It is unverifiable whether this is the work of one culprit or several.

The constable and the museum guards have reported an increase in foot traffic in the Kensington area from tourists, school students and locals. The museum, like many public institutions, has seen a dramatic increase in visitors in recent days, owing to the heavy rains, the flooding and ponding on many roads.

The museum has since reopened for public visits, albeit with additional precautions in place: museum officials have increased the security in the exhibit to deter further crime.

It is as well that this is so. It is highly improper, in the view of this newspaper, for learned institutions such as the Natural History Museum to be thus vandalised, and for public servants to be subjected to such senseless brutality. This affront is doubtless politically motivated. An attack on the museum is an attack on the global power it emblemises. Every effort must be made to discover and apprehend the perpetrators and deter future acts of barbarism.

"What do you make of it?" Holmes asked when I had finished reading.

"I can make neither head nor tail of the business," I replied, as my eyes wandered through the account again. "The culprit waits until after the museum closes to commit the crime. Was this even a burglary? He or she breaks into the museum, attacks a security guard, and leaves without stealing any of a number of priceless items. There is no evidence to implicate any party, so maybe the would-be thief was scared off by the response of the other security chap – what's his name... Merton? It seems as if no harm was done, other than a broken window and Wright's sore head. Why take such an interest?"

"Watson," Holmes reasoned, "you ought to examine the

printed word more carefully. Things are rarely as they seem when it comes to the criminal mind.

"I have a few conjectures," he continued. "But it is a fatal flaw to settle on one before we have all of the evidence. Let us trace over what we know. That the window was broken is unmistakable, but who is to say if the window was broken from the inside or the outside?"

"I confess that I do not follow."

"The glass shards were removed, perhaps with the best intentions, and as a result we cannot determine from which side the glass was broken. Suppose, Watson, that the culprit was concealed inside the museum after it closed, that he or she made the attack and then left through the window. The lack of mud at the scene would support this."

What does Holmes suspect that Watson does not?

"Surely the guards would have discovered the culprit in their patrols?"

"Let me trace more of the steps in my reasoning. What is the rationale for this burglary if not theft? The museum is well protected both within and without. Mr Merton, having discovered the unconscious Mr Wright, raises the alarm, whereupon several guards and a policeman soon join him at the scene. The museum surmises that no item has been stolen. What if the culprit's aim was never to steal from the museum?"

"I understand," I said. "But why? And who?"

"It would be unwise to speculate until we know more. I believe a visit to Kensington is in order. The weather has improved significantly, even if it is still muddy outside, and my limbs could use some unstiffening. Why don't we walk

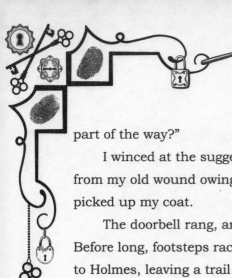

part of the way?"

I winced at the suggestion. All week, I had felt a dull ache from my old wound owing to the damp weather. I sighed and picked up my coat.

The doorbell rang, and we heard Mrs Hudson answer it. Before long, footsteps raced upstairs. A boy delivered a telegram to Holmes, leaving a trail of mud behind him, Mrs Hudson chasing after him with a broom, and Lydia after her with hers.

The message, like so many delivered to Baker Street, came from Inspector Lestrade, the famous detective who so often sought my friend's advice. But its contents had a curious effect on Holmes. It brought an unfamiliar furrow to his brow.

"Curious," he muttered. "Why meet him there?"

Holmes quickly dispatched a message with the urchin, and I was too good a sport to pry into what he wrote. It was clear that Lestrade's missive was like none other, and our plans were to be postponed. He handed me the following message, which meant little to my untrained eyes:

POSTAL TELEGRAPH   COMMERCIAL CABLES

TELEGRAM

Telegraph-Cable   transmits and delivers this message subject to the terms and conditions printed on the back of this blank.

COUNTER NUMBER.	TIME FILED.	CHECK.	
	M.		

Send the following message, without repeating, subject to the terms and conditions printed on the back hereof, which are hereby agreed to.

FOR HOLMES STOP I REQUIRE ASSISTANCE
STOP NEED YOU TO READE CAREFULLY STOP
CASE INVOLVING CHILDREN STOP HEAVY IS THE
HEAD THAT WEARS THE CROWN STOP LET US
MEET AT THE PUB STOP EMBARK ON SOONEST
DEPARTURE STOP YOURS LESTRADE STOP

Holmes glanced at his watch, returned to his armchair, curled up his long legs and seemed to have forgotten me altogether. I resumed my breakfast. So overwhelming was my curiosity that I had little idea what I was eating, much less what it tasted like.

A quarter hour passed and for the second time that morning Holmes woke from his reverie. I looked to him quizzically as he noted, "You are applying butter to your bacon, my dear Watson."

My face flushed. To mitigate some of my embarrassment, I asked, "Where are we to meet Lestrade?"

"My presence is most urgently needed in Finchley," he continued. "Yours would be most valued if you can spare it. That Lestrade sends a telegram is commonplace: he is baffled so much of the time. He knows that I do not indulge in pleasantries. There must be something gravely amiss. I promise to reveal everything I know on our way."

"Finchley?" I inquired of Holmes. "How did you get that from the telegram? It mentions nothing of the sort."

"Ah, Watson," said Holmes. "Lestrade is a cautious fellow. He feels the need to conceal the location. Why? I'm sure he has his reasons. Look carefully at the telegram, specifically at the first letter of each sentence. It tells us where to go, yet the message would be meaningless if it were to fall into the wrong hands."

"I see it now," I said. "But why all the secrecy? And what shall we do about the museum burglary?"

"I have given instructions to Gregson who will act on our

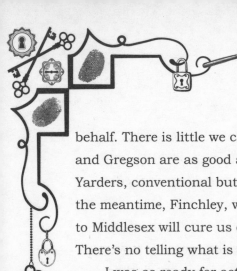

behalf. There is little we can do until we know more. Lestrade and Gregson are as good as can be expected of Scotland Yarders, conventional but efficient and quick to respond. In the meantime, Finchley, with its glorious greens, awaits. A trip to Middlesex will cure us of the springtime blues. Pack a bag. There's no telling what is ahead of us."

I was as ready for action as ever, but Holmes was even quicker to the door than I. As we passed the coat tree, I nodded to the cap on the uppermost rack.

"I am not wearing the cap," said Holmes.

"You have a reputation to keep," I insisted.

"I did not, if you recall, wear a deerstalker in the entire Ferguson affair. In fact, you got me the cap because you thought it'd be humorous."

I was determined to have my way, and Holmes deduced from the steely determination in my eyes that this would not be a battle won lightly.

"All right, Watson," he said. "I will wear the cap if you can pass a little test of mine. I shall pose a riddle, and you get but one guess. If you fail, you will not mention my cap again."

"Agreed," I said, ready to give Holmes his just deserts.

We shook on it.

"In my youth, I stood tall and straight, but – as time passed – I became short and stubby as I aged. But tears shed for my lost youth do not quickly fade. Knowing that my life provided clarity to those around me eases my fears of passing into the darkness. What am I?"

What is the answer to the riddle?

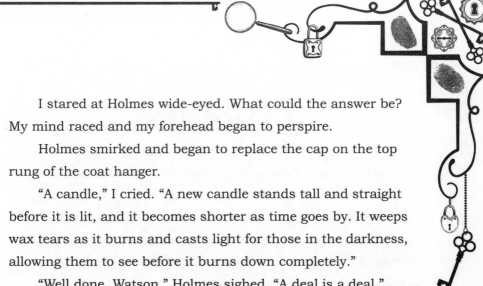

I stared at Holmes wide-eyed. What could the answer be? My mind raced and my forehead began to perspire.

Holmes smirked and began to replace the cap on the top rung of the coat hanger.

"A candle," I cried. "A new candle stands tall and straight before it is lit, and it becomes shorter as time goes by. It weeps wax tears as it burns and casts light for those in the darkness, allowing them to see before it burns down completely."

"Well done, Watson," Holmes sighed. "A deal is a deal."

He placed the hat on his head. We strolled down the stairs and marched out of 221B Baker Street.

"Watson, we face two methods to get to Finchley to make our meeting with Lestrade: by train or by carriage. Which form of travel should we take? There is clearly a better option."

If you think Holmes and Watson should travel by train, turn to page 31.

If you think Holmes and Watson should travel by cab, turn to page 69.

What method of travel should they choose?

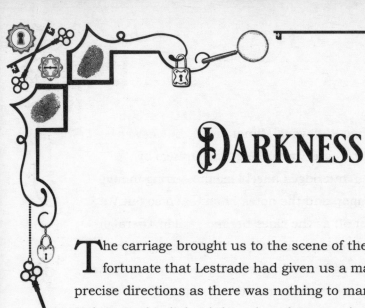

DARKNESS

The carriage brought us to the scene of the tragedy. It was fortunate that Lestrade had given us a map with such precise directions as there was nothing to mark the location. Holmes and I alighted the cab and surveyed our surroundings. The mud stuck instantly to our shoes and the bottom of our trousers. At times, Holmes held out his hand to prevent me from stepping on particular spots, though they looked unremarkable to me. At others, he swung and turned, following the contours of footprints discernible only to him.

"I have a good idea of both Miss Forman's and the culprit's movements. The carriage stopped here, where you are standing," Holmes began.

"Miss Forman got off and walked to the front of the carriage, but not directly. That's probably on account of the heavy wind and rain. She stood beside the driver for some time: you can see the remnant of a print here, near where I am standing. The tree sheltered it – do you see? Here is another set of prints. They vanished into the grass just steps away from where the Bracewell carriage stopped. We can only assume that they belong to the culprit."

"There is something I don't understand," he added. "The mystery isn't quite what I had expected."

"How do you mean?"

"I have a working hypothesis, which I shall share with you before the sun is set. Come, Watson, let us find the quickest way

What road should they take to get to the main gate of Westwood Manor?

to Westwood Manor."

"It would be quickest to go by Totteridge Lane," I said, referring to my map and the notes I had taken so far. We set off as the skies began to clear. There was birdsong in the air, and with it, my spirits soared. The two-mile stroll passed without event, and we soon arrived at a wrought-iron gate emblazoned with the Bracewell coat of arms.

As we ventured through it, we came across a small iron map of the different locations on the estate. I made a quick rubbing of it *(page 18)*, both to prevent our getting lost and to keep a memento of this mystery.

After a fifteen-minute walk, the large, twelfth-century house loomed before us. Westwood Manor was a beautiful estate that bespoke simplicity and practicality. The immense windows glistened in the late afternoon sun and several of them were open, allowing in the fresh air. The stone steps up to the main entrance were immaculately clean. I felt rather embarrassed to dirty them with my muddy boots, though Holmes shared none of my inhibitions. A footman opened the door and led us immediately into the hallway.

It was clear that Lord Bracewell was expecting us. The footman left us to our own devices while he announced our arrival. We took in the immensity of the house and the curious array of artwork and ornaments around us that must have been accrued from generations of travel: boomerangs and dillybags were displayed beside shields, didgeridoos and Nazcan pottery.

"What a trove!" I exclaimed. "I wonder if our culprit could have been after these artefacts. Some of these pots and weapons

Farmland

Pigpens

Rock mounds

Servant's house

Westwood Manor

Cemetery

Lake

Forest glen

Crypt

Gardens

Cricket field

Gazebo

Stables

Lavender maze

Fountain

Hunting fields

Estate gates

must be priceless!"

Holmes put his finger to his lips. "As yet, we do not know who knows what. Is the whole household aware that the children are missing? And that Mullins is dead? Anyone could be complicit in either crime.

"Hm. There is something amiss here."

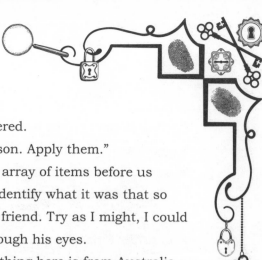

"What is it, Holmes?" I wondered.

"You know my methods, Watson. Apply them."

I looked at the array of items before us but could not identify what it was that so troubled my friend. Try as I might, I could not see through his eyes.

What is amiss that Holmes has detected since his arrival?

"Everything here is from Australia, so why would pottery from the Nazca culture of Peru be included?" he said, as he picked up a pot.

"The Bracewells are global traders," I said. "It is natural that the pieces in their collection should come from all corners of the world."

"Perhaps," said Holmes. "But is it not odd that there is only the one pot?"

The footman returned just then. "Have you been to Westwood Manor before?" he asked.

"No," I replied. "We have never had the privilege."

"Then please allow me to give you a tour."

He led us through a maze of rooms into a dining hall, where he stopped abruptly.

"The shell of this house dates from the twelfth century. Evidently, parts of it have been extended and renovated over the years. The Bracewell line is one of the oldest families in this area. Portraits of the Bracewells date back many generations and have recently been returned from a major conservation project. The pictures hang in the main gallery on either side of the family coat, which was granted to the first Lord Bracewell by William II, son of William the Conqueror. The portraits here are of the more recent generations."

He motioned to the back of the hall where a large stained-glass window stood proudly. It was a glorious affair: a single ship docked at the centre with water surrounding it.

"This window celebrates the family's connection to global trade. It's on the north wall, appropriately because the scene includes the North Star, which has led many a ship to safety. The present Lord Bracewell's great-grandfather hangs behind us, above the entrance to the hall; Bracewell's grandfather hangs to the right, near the British swords and shields he collected; his father hangs in front of us, underneath the window in the place of honour; and the current Lord Bracewell hangs to the left, amidst some of the artefacts he acquired on his travels, including a collection of hand-drawn maps. He has always said that these are a source of inspiration for him."

Holmes was no connoisseur of art, but he nevertheless studied the portraits. We looked at the Bracewells and the resemblance between generations was uncanny: the devilish grandfather's appearance registered meanness, his eyes glaring at us as if we were intruders. The present Bracewell was a tall and lean man, handsome, and appeared to be in his late twenties. The painting must have been made when he first took ownership of the estate. He stood in front of a fireplace outfitted in formal dress complete with sword, hilt in his right hand and blade lightly resting in his left. The Bracewell family coat of arms hung from a banner behind him.

The footman led us into a well-aired study, a room that exemplified cleanliness, comfort and respectability, and told us that Lord Bracewell would be with us momentarily. The wooden surfaces glimmered beneath the polish. The mantelpiece held only a few select ornaments and pictures; shelf after shelf of books lined the walls. Holmes noted a peculiarity about the placement of one of the books. I noticed nothing out of the ordinary. After pressing Holmes, he curtly observed that the books were arranged neither alphabetically by author nor by title. Knowing my friend's methodical nature, his disorganisation notwithstanding, I sympathised with his concern.

Our surroundings made me feel terribly out of place, but my companion was lost in his thoughts. Lord Bracewell entered and motioned us to take a seat. He was a number of years older than his portrait, but his face remained handsome, if aged by time and grief, and his frame was still that of a natural athlete.

"Dr Watson," he addressed me. "I must congratulate you on your wonderful account of the Jefferson affair. I have been quite unable to put it down. I have since shared it with my children – to their absolute delight. Can we hope for a sequel?"

I was not ashamed to say that I was pleased to hear his compliment. Before I could answer he turned to my friend: "And Mr Holmes, I have long known of your extraordinary powers, even before I read the fine narrative. I have heard, through the grapevine, how you helped poor Reginald Musgrave with his family matter. It is an honour to meet you both and I know that my children are in the best possible hands now that Holmes and Watson are on the case!"

Holmes bowed.

"My household and I are at your disposal and we would be proud to host you during your investigations."

"Thank you very much for your hospitality. We will do our best to be worthy of your kindness. Can you tell us about the late Harry Mullins? He has been in your employment for the past five years, correct?"

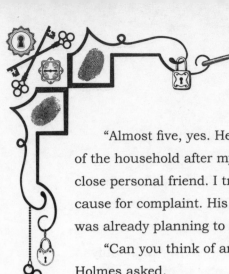

"Almost five, yes. He became an indispensable member of the household after my wife's death and I considered him a close personal friend. I trusted him in all matters and never had cause for complaint. His death is doubly unfortunate now, as he was already planning to leave us to care for his aging parents."

"Can you think of anyone who would wish him harm?" Holmes asked.

"No one at all. He has never had a quarrel in all the time I've known him. I had planned to set him up in a small business, a shop near his parents' home."

"How would you describe the children's relationship with Mullins?"

"They trusted him implicitly, as I did. Time and again, he proved himself a most capable servant. I relied on him to represent me on numerous occasions. However, the same could not be said for our dog, Spot: he detested the man and proved difficult to manage around him without considerable efforts."

"Is there any reason why, that you know of?"

"None whatsoever."

"Do you have any idea where the children might be?"

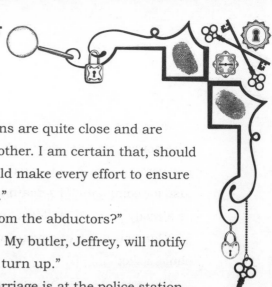

"No, I am afraid not. The twins are quite close and are naturally very protective of each other. I am certain that, should one be threatened, the other would make every effort to ensure no harm came to their other half."

"Have you heard anything from the abductors?"

"Nothing has been delivered. My butler, Jeffrey, will notify me immediately should anything turn up."

"Lestrade tells us that the carriage is at the police station, where we will also find Mullins's body."

"The station is a thirty-minute walk from this house, not far from where the carriage was discovered. You can take a more direct route and save some minutes if you leave by the north gate. Jeffrey will provide you with anything you need." Lord Bracewell shook our hands before ringing the bell. The signet ring on his finger chimed as it came into contact with the metal bell. "Can I make two requests?"

"By all means," Holmes replied.

"Can you keep me abreast of any and all developments? Since my wife's death, the children are all I have."

"I promise to recover the children," said Holmes. "And your second request?"

"Can you arrange to have the carriage returned here once you complete your investigation? I assume that they are holding it for that exact purpose."

"Yes, of course," said Holmes.

As we waited for Jeffrey, Holmes studied the bookshelves again and made some notes in his pocketbook.

"Holmes, what have you spotted?" I asked.

"What caught my eye initially was that there are nine books on the shelf and only one of them is upside down. What do you

see, Watson?"

"Well, Holmes, I see a collection of books, nothing more."

"Watson, my dear boy. Do you recall the telegram from Lestrade? With that in mind, look again."

I looked a second time, and felt foolish for staring at a bookshelf for as long as I did. In order, the books were *Wuthering Heights* by Emily Bronte, *Emma* by Jane Austen, *Moby Dick* by Herman Melville, *Italy* by Germaine de Stael, *The Scarlet Letter* by Nathaniel Hawthorne, *School Days* by Tom Brown, *On Liberty* by John Stuart Mill (which was upside down), *Oliver Twist* by Charles Dickens and *Uncle Tom's Cabin* by Harriet Beecher Stowe.

Does the bookshelf hide a message?

Then the solution appeared to me.

"It says 'we miss you', using the first letters of the titles. *On Liberty* threw me off, as it is upside down, but we are meant to use the Y, and not the O, for that title. It would appear the children miss their father?"

At that moment, Jeffrey arrived.

The butler led us out of the house. His behaviour made it clear that, while he would comply with his employer's instructions, he took no pleasure in them.

On our walk towards the police station, Jeffrey looked constantly at his immaculately polished shoes and avoided puddles as best he could. The station was only a mile and a half from Lord Bracewell's home, but in following Jeffrey from alleyway to alleyway once we returned to Totteridge, I lost all sense of direction.

"Here," he said. A plaque indicated our destination. The

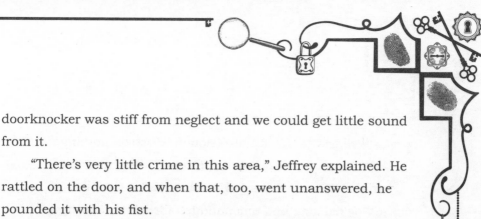

doorknocker was stiff from neglect and we could get little sound from it.

"There's very little crime in this area," Jeffrey explained. He rattled on the door, and when that, too, went unanswered, he pounded it with his fist.

The knock was answered by a potbellied constable, whose eyes surveyed each of us in turn. "Wha' you want?"

"We are here to see the carriage that was brought in last night," said Holmes.

"What carriage? I don't know nothing about one."

"We were assured it is being kept at this station."

"By who? Who are you?"

Jeffrey stepped in to introduce us. Holmes's name had an immediate effect on the constable. His annoyance was replaced by awe.

"Mr Sherlock Holmes," he cried. "What brings you to our humble station?"

"As I said, I hope to see the carriage that was brought in. I would also very much like to see the corpse of Harry Mullins."

"Certainly. The coroner has yet to arrive."

"Perfect," Holmes said. "My colleague here was an army doctor and I am sure he can tell us anything we need to know about the cause and time of death."

I blushed at the compliment, though Jeffrey and the constable – the only police officer in the station – looked at me dubiously. The officer led us through a back door into a courtyard, where a lone carriage stood, with the two horses in a makeshift stable to the side.

"I am sorry to show it to you in such a disgraceful state. It is splattered with mud and we have yet to clean it," the

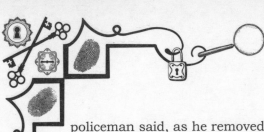

policeman said, as he removed a towel from his pocket and began to wipe the carriage exterior.

"Of that I am very glad!" said Holmes, and the man desisted.

Holmes circled the carriage, by turns squatting and stretching his long legs and noting marks on the woodwork here and there. The Bracewell coat of arms, like so much of the carriage, was coated in dried mud. Holmes stopped beside the driver's seat and scrutinised its surface. He removed from inside the carriage a burnt-out Bolivar cigar and a small cloth sack, taking note of the crest carved onto the panel behind which Miss Forman had hidden her diary. He broke into a satisfied smile. I tried to imitate Holmes, but the carriage was, to my naked eye, almost entirely devoid of interest.

Holmes's examination of the passenger's seat was far briefer. He disappeared for but a moment, before he re-emerged to remark: "All the prints have been obliterated. It really is too bad. However, Watson, I have noted one item of interest. Do you recall that when we arrived at the scene of the crime there was a strange imprint in the mud where we initially stood?"

I stared blankly at Holmes.

"There was the imprint of the bow of a key left in the mud near the foot of the carriage steps. If you recall, I stopped you from stepping on it; that is what I was reviewing. The imprint is a match for the upper corner of the crest on the carriage. Evidently, a key was used to lock the carriage from the outside, Watson, and we need to determine who possessed it. If Miss Forman locked the children in the carriage, then how did the children get out of it?"

We returned to the station, where the policeman took us through to an office. A lone corpse was laid out on a table. I shall never forget the expression on Harry Mullins's face. He was a man of undefinable age: he could have been anywhere between thirty-five and fifty-five. He wore his raven black hair like a lion's mane. But it was the anger and terror in his eyes that imprinted themselves upon me. The contortion of Mullins's rigid face made his physical features almost unidentifiable. I had seen many a corpse during my time in the army, but I could not wait to flee that room and get out into the fresh air. It was clear that he had died of a gun wound – he had been shot in the chest – and I could not see why Holmes examined his clenched fists and open lips so closely.

Upon completing his examination, Holmes moved to a small adjacent table on which were laid out the dead man's personal effects:

- Five matches and four cigarettes in a gold cigarette case with the Bracewell coat of arms
- Four sovereigns and £20 in notes.
- A gold ring
- A note with strange symbols on it, signed by 'M'
- A few sugar cubes wrapped up in a handkerchief

"How very curious," said Holmes. "One of these items doesn't make sense with what we've discovered so far; another is missing based on what we've been told; and yet another should be here, although it is nowhere to be found."

"What do you mean, Holmes?" I asked.

"The sugar cubes, Watson," said Holmes. "There were

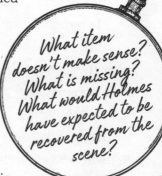

What item doesn't make sense? What is missing? What would Holmes have expected to be recovered from the scene?

sugar cubes, likely as a treat for the horses, in a handkerchief in Mullins's pocket. Why are they still in squares despite the pouring rain? Yet another thread to follow up on! And where is the locket containing the picture of Mullins's fiancée? Lestrade told us about it. Finally, Mullins was shot, but no casing was found at the scene."

"I have seen all that there is to see," he said at last to the constable, after noting down the symbols found in the note from 'M'. "Jeffrey can return the carriage to Westwood Manor if you have no further need for it."

We wished the officer goodbye and bid farewell to the impatient Jeffrey, who returned with the constable to the courtyard.

As we left the station, Holmes showed me the message that was found on Mullins's body and asked what I could make of it:

<E<F >FƎ◻ >E ⅂⅃< ⊓⅃V
◻>⅂⌐Ѓ◻⅃.

Ѓ ⴸ⅂ᴸᴸ V◻◻ <E< VEE◻.

— *M*

At first glance, some of the symbols here looked like mathematics, but after looking at it for a few seconds, it dawned on me as to where I had seen this before. Some of the officers I had served under in Afghanistan encoded their messages this way, using the Masonic cipher.

I started sketching in my journal. After a minute or two, I

What does the message from M say?

was able to figure out what 'M' had to say to Mullins. It was a threat, and a deadly one considering the circumstances.

"It says 'Your time to pay has expired. I will see you soon'," I said to Holmes.

"It appears that Mullins owed money to the wrong person," said Holmes. "We shall have to see if the threat was carried out by M, or if Mullins had other enemies.

If you are yet to visit George Hewitt, the postman, turn to page 176.

If you have already visited George Hewitt, turn to page 37.

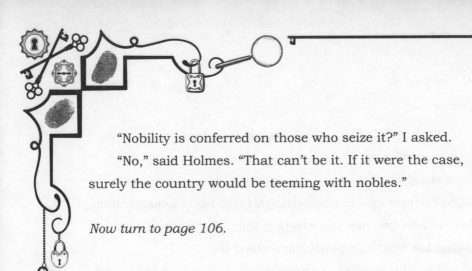

"Nobility is conferred on those who seize it?" I asked.

"No," said Holmes. "That can't be it. If it were the case, surely the country would be teeming with nobles."

Now turn to page 106.

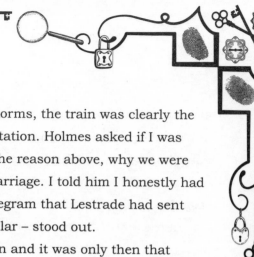

Due to the weeklong rainstorms, the train was clearly the more efficient mode of transportation. Holmes asked if I was able to deduce, other than for the reason above, why we were travelling by train and not by carriage. I told him I honestly had no idea, and he gave me the telegram that Lestrade had sent and asked me what – in particular – stood out.

I studied the telegram again and it was only then that I noticed the spelling error in the third line: "Need you to reade carefully."

"Of course," I said. "Read E carefully: the line starting with the capital letter E. 'Embark on soonest departure' tells us to take the next train. That's why you sat back down after getting the telegram. The next train wasn't scheduled to depart until rather later this morning! At least that gave me time to finish my breakfast."

As we made our way to the station, Holmes was cheerful and made frequent comments regarding passers-by. There was no knowing whether any of his observations were right, but my faith in the detective was implicit.

We arrived at the station just as our train stopped on the platform. Passengers hurried to board as others hurried to disembark. We walked alongside the train, only to find carriage after carriage filled. It was clear that many others had hoped to avail themselves of the sunshine and head out of the city. We found plenty of seating available in the rearmost car. We pushed in and sat down and the train left the station. An older man with a dark beard and pale face looked as if he meant to follow us into the carriage, but he stopped and stood at the door, studying us for a while.

We passed the time talking about the inspector we were

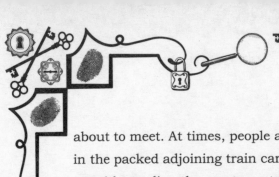

about to meet. At times, people appeared at the window in the packed adjoining train carriage, yet they withdrew, notwithstanding the empty seats and breathing room around us. I shrugged and returned to our conversation, happy for the space and to be able to speak without fear of being overheard.

At the station before Finchley, I saw the same man with the dark beard and pale face disembark from the carriage in front of us onto the platform. He paused by the door to our carriage, and again stared at us for a few moments, seemingly trying to place our faces before going on his way. Was this, perhaps, a reader of my brochure, who lacked the nerve to meet the great detective? This suspicion was uppermost on my mind as the train slowly pulled out of the station.

We pulled into Finchley and got up to disembark. However, the door from our carriage to the platform refused to open. I struggled but was unsuccessful, even as the engine made noises to leave the station.

How does Watson get them out of the carriage?

"Holmes," I cried. "We are trapped! We need to find our way out of this carriage if we are to make our meeting. Help me look around and find a way out of here!"

After searching the luggage rack, I noticed that partially hidden under an adjoining seat was a crowbar. I grabbed it and prised the doors a few inches apart and, together with Holmes, we pulled the doors open far enough to escape onto the platform. I handed the crowbar to the astonished platform attendant and we made our way down the stairs.

"How unlucky we were to be trapped," I said. "We should have informed the attendant that the doors were defective to prevent other poor souls from being locked in."

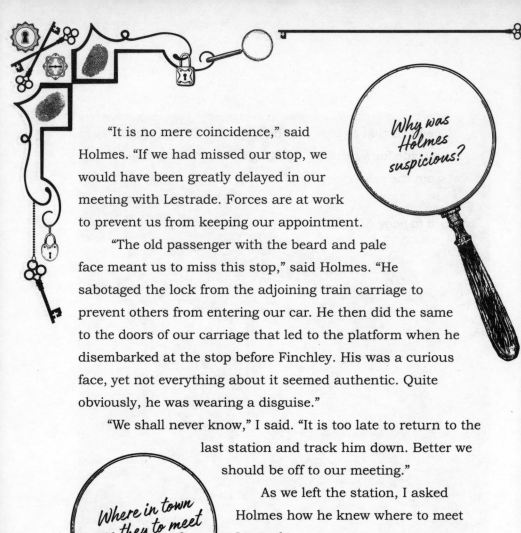

"It is no mere coincidence," said Holmes. "If we had missed our stop, we would have been greatly delayed in our meeting with Lestrade. Forces are at work to prevent us from keeping our appointment.

Why was Holmes suspicious?

"The old passenger with the beard and pale face meant us to miss this stop," said Holmes. "He sabotaged the lock from the adjoining train carriage to prevent others from entering our car. He then did the same to the doors of our carriage that led to the platform when he disembarked at the stop before Finchley. His was a curious face, yet not everything about it seemed authentic. Quite obviously, he was wearing a disguise."

"We shall never know," I said. "It is too late to return to the last station and track him down. Better we should be off to our meeting."

As we left the station, I asked Holmes how he knew where to meet Lestrade.

Where in town are they to meet Lestrade?

"Why Watson," he replied, "we have all the information we need in the telegram. Did you not deduce where in Finchley our meeting with Lestrade is to take place?"

I confessed that the message was mysterious to my untrained eyes.

"The telegram is as cryptic regarding the precise location where we are to meet him as it is in pinpointing Finchley. The location resides in the rest of the telegram. 'Heavy is the head that wears the crown' is an echo of Shakespeare's Henry IV, part 2: 'Uneasy lies the head that wears a crown'.

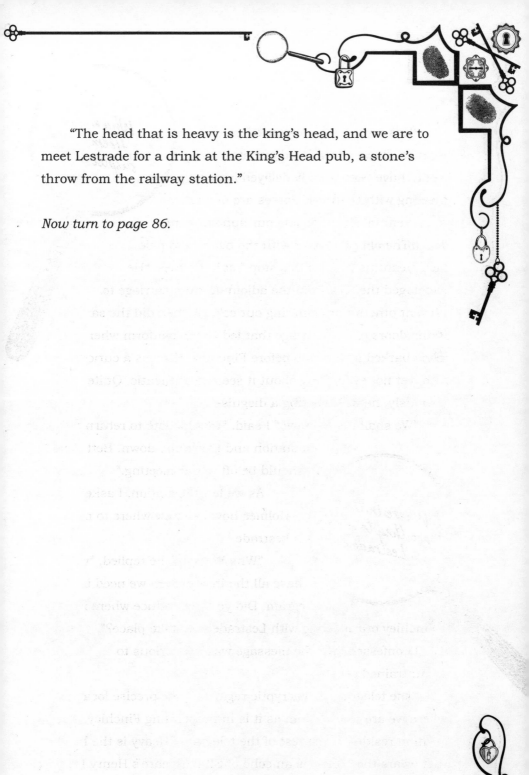

"The head that is heavy is the king's head, and we are to meet Lestrade for a drink at the King's Head pub, a stone's throw from the railway station."

Now turn to page 86.

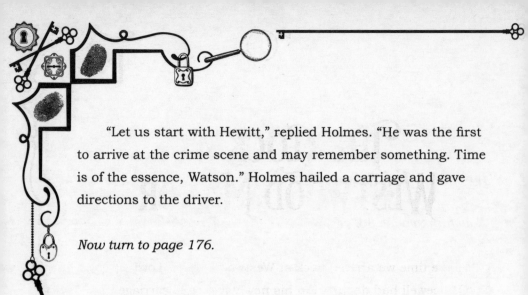

"Let us start with Hewitt," replied Holmes. "He was the first to arrive at the crime scene and may remember something. Time is of the essence, Watson." Holmes hailed a carriage and gave directions to the driver.

Now turn to page 176.

THE CLOCK AT WESTWOOD MANOR

By the time we arrived back at Westwood Manor Lord Bracewell had departed in his newly returned carriage. He left an apologetic note:

> Dear Mr Holmes and Dr Watson,
>
> My sincerest apologies to you both – I have been called to London on urgent business and shall return later this evening or tomorrow morning. Please be welcome at Westwood Manor in the meantime.
>
> I have instructed Mrs Clemens and Jeffrey to see to your needs. They will also make ready other members of household staff should you wish to ask them questions.
>
> Yours faithfully,
> Philip Bracewell

After we dined, Jeffrey the butler took us to the third floor, where the guest quarters exuded as much warmth and comfort as can be found anywhere.

The room had two large beds covered with thick, dark blue, down comforters, a sturdy wooden dresser with four drawers and a small empty wardrobe, complete with hangers. A small square table and two chairs were placed near the window, from which there was a beautiful view of the estate. A small chess set sat upon the table, yet it was clear from the

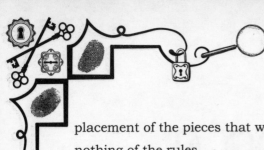

placement of the pieces that whoever had set the board knew nothing of the rules.

A vase with flowers from the garden stood atop a small, round table next to the door. The room was finished with a large fireplace decorated with a series of realistic-looking embossed plaster vines coloured green that appeared to sprout from the floor around the fireplace, grow up the side and into the ceiling. A copy of *Jane Eyre*, with a bookmark, could be seen sitting on the mantelpiece.

After spending so many hours outdoors, it was reassuring to find oneself inside the house once more, but it was in this restive mode that the pain from my old shoulder injury returned. Holmes saw me wincing and observed:

"The thirst for action is in you, as it is in me."

I replied that I was perfectly content in my seat with a book.

"Am I wrong in thinking that, in all the hours that we have spent together, you did not once think about your old wound? Perhaps a spot of tea will help you relax and ease the pangs of your injury."

Holmes stood up and strode to the door. He turned the knob and pulled, but it would not budge. "It is locked," said Holmes, as he looked around the room. "I do not see a key, nor any way to summon help."

We began searching the room for a bell that would ring in the servants' quarters. None could be found. Then Holmes went to the mantelpiece and started leafing through the novel. He came to the bookmark, which he picked up and examined. He smiled after his short examination and passed it over to me.

The bookmark was covered in childish script with the

words "Poor Bertha" and a series of four numbers set apart by columns. Each column was headed with a letter:

C	P	S	W
1	7	1	9
11	3	5	5
10	10	1	3
20	15	1	3
7	8	2	34
2	25	9	23s

"I don't understand," I said after trying to make a connection between the numbers and the columns.

Holmes laughed. "Ah, Watson. It appears we are the victims of a youthful prank. The children apparently like to play tricks on their guests by locking them in the room and seeing if they are smart enough to figure out how to leave. The bookmark and this copy of *Jane Eyre* will tell us what to do. Bertha was a character locked in a room on the third floor. What cheeky little devils!"

"That is all well and good, Holmes," I said. "But we are still locked in this room."

"All in good time, Watson," he said. "Give me a few moments and I'm sure I can find the answer to their puzzle. It's important to know that Charlotte Brontë uses a lot of semicolons and hyphens in her writing, so we should take things associated with these items of punctuation as separate ideas."

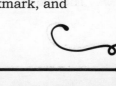

How does Holmes escape the locked room?

Holmes studied the numbers on the bookmark, and

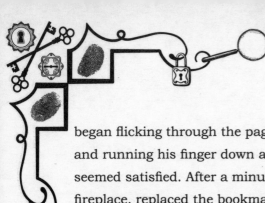

began flicking through the pages, stopping at certain points and running his finger down and then across the print until he seemed satisfied. After a minute or two, he walked over to the fireplace, replaced the bookmark and returned the volume to the mantelpiece.

He moved to the left of the fireplace, counted to the third vine and pulled on it. Instead of the plaster breaking off in his hand, the vine astonishingly pulled away from the wall and then snapped back into place.

Holmes returned to the table and sat down.

"How did you know the vine was really a bell?" I asked.

"The series of numbers on the bookmark directed me to use the sequence to look for chapter, then paragraph, then sentence and then word. Each sequence of numbers corresponds to a specific word. Finding all six gives you the message, 'To ring bell, pull third vines' and the scored-through letter 's' next to the 23 tells us to remove the 's' in the word you find; so 'vines' becomes 'vine'. That's how I knew the vine was a bell to summon one of the servants. I'm sure the butler just forgot to give us that bit of information."

After Holmes had completed his explanation, the doorknob turned and a maid entered the room with an apologetic look.

"I'm so sorry," she said. "The butler has tried to fix the lock multiple times, but the children always find some way to undo his work. You don't know how many times I've come up to the third floor to clean or put something away only to find our guests pounding on this door and begging to be freed. This room is solidly built and far enough away from the main staircase to prevent anyone from hearing shouts unless we're on this floor a few rooms away. How long have you been trying to free yourselves?"

"For only about five minutes," said Holmes. "And do not worry about it. I found the challenge to be a delightful distraction. Might we have some tea, however?"

"Only five minutes!" exclaimed the maid. "You are a genius, surely! I will fetch your tea immediately." She left and – pausing at the open door – pushed it all the way open to the wall before she left the room with a smile.

She returned ten minutes later with our tea and set it on the table in front of us, moving the chess set off to the side with care not to disturb the pieces. It was clear from the glances she stole at us that Holmes, at least, piqued her awe and curiosity.

"Excuse me," he said to the maid, "can you please tell us the time?"

I looked at him in askance. A stately grandfather clock stood in the hall directly across from us and its rhythmic ticking was, if anything, distracting.

"If you don't mind me saying so, Mr Holmes, you are most observant," said the maid.

Holmes bowed his head slightly, but I could see that he was pleased with the compliment.

"You see, Watson," he said, "this clock is moving rather faster than a regular clock. The musician in me believes that an hour on this clock is an hour and a half on a timepiece moving at normal speed."

What is the answer to Holmes's puzzle?

"You are exactly right, Mr Holmes," said the maid.

"So, Watson," continued Holmes, "if the clock chimes at noon today and is the correct time, at what time will the clock once again chime the hour correctly?"

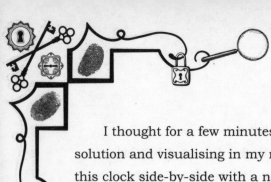

I thought for a few minutes, ignoring the mathematical solution and visualising in my mind the turning of the hands of this clock side-by-side with a normal one. After a few minutes, I confidently said: "At noon tomorrow this clock will also be striking twelve, but for midnight on the next day."

"Well done, Watson!" said Holmes. "Now, my dear, might we ask you some questions?"

The maid paused for a second before curiosity got the better of her. "Is it true that you can read minds?"

"No," my friend said. "Such powers are not of this world. My gifts are confined to this one, no more and no less."

It was clear that the maid did not believe him.

"But you knew from the very beginning what was afoot with the Jefferson Hope case!"

"Ah! That was elementary. Just as it's clearly visible that you are a maid by morning and a writer by night."

"How did you know?" she cried.

"I suspected from the way you cover your hands with your apron. Are they stained by ink?"

"Yes, I had tried to wash it off, but I write every night religiously just before bedtime. There's always too much to do during the day."

"Then you will, no doubt, benefit from the wisdom of Watson, to whom the credit for the Jefferson affair rightly belongs. Watson prioritises the romantic and sensational over the concrete facts and my deductive powers. Neither of us, for example, has ever lain eyes on Lucy or can vouch that she was beautiful or pale-faced."

"Now, just a minute, Holmes," I cried. "It is clear from Hope's account—"

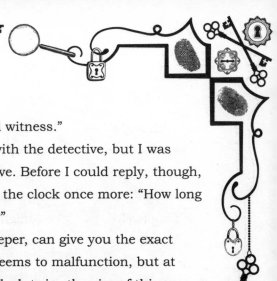

"Hope is hardly an impartial witness."

It was impossible to argue with the detective, but I was determined to defend my narrative. Before I could reply, though, Holmes directed our attention to the clock once more: "How long has the clock been out of repair?"

"Mrs Clemens, our housekeeper, can give you the exact dates. I'd say this clock always seems to malfunction, but at least it operates. A grandfather clock twice the size of this one is downstairs at the end of the main hall. That one has *never* run properly.

"When Mrs Clemens showed me around the house after I first arrived last month, she told me that every few decades, going back to the current lord's grandfather, the Bracewell at the head of the family would seek the advice of clockmakers. It has been inspected by generations of experts, but the verdict has always been that the clock is beyond repair – without huge reconstruction and possible damage to the artwork. And so that clock has never been fixed."

Holmes mused for a while. He then walked out of the room into the hallway to the mistimed grandfather clock. He opened the door to the clock and inspected its inner workings – after asking for the maid's permission, of course. He remarked to me how it was unlike any other clock he had seen.

There was a series of gears behind the clockface that seemed to be working relatively well, considering that something appeared to be missing from the centre, and it was this that caused the clock to run more slowly than it was supposed to. Above and below the main mechanism were several gears that we assumed would be the right fit for the empty space, but upon trying them all, my friend said, "Interesting. It appears that the

selection of gears on the door that are available to fill this space do not meet the requirements of the rest of the set. No wonder it's been in disrepair for as long as you remember.

Can you fix the clock?

"But, if we try this one and place it here on top of this other one…"

Holmes stopped the pendulum, took the top left and bottom right of the four gears from the inside of the door panel and set one atop the other. As he restarted the clock, he said, "That should do the trick quite nicely."

Immediately, even I could tell the difference in that the ticking was faster than it had been.

"Thank you, Mr Holmes!" said the maid. "Now, what questions did you want to ask of me?"

"How well did you know Harry Mullins?" Holmes asked.

"I don't wish to speak poorly of the dead," she replied, "but Mullins was very quarrelsome. He had a mighty row with Mrs Clemens a fortnight ago."

"What was the dispute regarding?" I asked.

"Mullins had some gambling debts." The maid hesitated before continuing: "I remember it as if it were yesterday: one morning, just a couple of weeks after I joined the house, two collectors came in through the kitchen door and asked for Mullins. He was elsewhere on the property and I was alone with the cook."

"How much did he owe?"

"Nearly a thousand pounds! One man said that they should leave and come back later and speak with Mullins privately, but the other said the sum was too large to wait any longer."

I whistled, while Holmes continued: "Did you learn who the collectors represented?"

"In a way, yes, but not exactly. They told me to fetch Mullins and to tell him that they represent 'M'. When I asked who 'M' was, they told me to do as I was instructed. I was happy to leave their presence but feared for the cook being left alone with them, so I ran out of the house to look for him. I found him on the road down near the fountain coming up to the house. He returned with me directly and he drew them out of the kitchen for a long conversation."

She hesitated before continuing: "I listened through the keyhole, as they do in detective stories, but I heard absolutely nothing."

"Does Lord Bracewell know of this bad business? Surely it makes an argument against his taking charge of the children," Holmes said.

"Mrs Clemens tells me that the master had lent Mullins some money a few times in the past, but I assume that a debt this substantial was one Mullins would not willingly have let his employer know about. Mullins may have been rough in appearance and he had not a friend in the world, but he was another man altogether when he was with the children.

"I am too bold – Mrs Clemens always tells me as much – but there was no caregiver for the children as good as he. He was always playing games with them and trying to teach them new ones. I think the most recent game was chess on this very set. He even came up with a little story to help them understand how the board is set up and how the pieces move. The children thought it too boring and created a story of their own. If you look underneath the board, you'll see yet another example of how their imagination runs."

I reached over and pulled the slip of paper that was showing from underneath the chessboard. The story was as follows:

Our Lady usually starts on a square of her own colour, but not here. Almost all of the foot soldiers are stationed correctly, but the Rook is one space ahead of its usual resting place. The King remains by his Queen's side, yet she confessed her love for the other King to the man standing next to her. The King was banging his head against the wall while his spiritual advisor looked on, wondering what brought upon his frustration. And the Knights horses were grazing next to a Pawn.

"What an inventive story," I said.

"Can you figure out how to represent their story by placing the pieces on the board?" asked Holmes.

"It's a logic puzzle," I said. "It is simply a matter of following directions and determining which puzzle pieces are referenced by the vague descriptions."

Can you match the chessboard to the story? Use the blank chessboard on page 222.

I worked for a few moments and restarted only twice, but in the end I placed the pieces properly and looked at them triumphantly.

The maid smiled a sad smile. "The children seemed to blossom under the care of Mullins. They could have had no better protector.

"Last winter, Bracewell and Mullins took the children

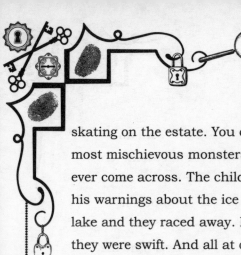

skating on the estate. You don't know the children: they are the most mischievous monsters – I mean, darlings – that you will ever come across. The children would not heed the master or his warnings about the ice not being safe in the middle of the lake and they raced away. Mullins followed as best he could, but they were swift. And all at once, the ice gave away and they fell into the water. Without a moment's thought for his own safety, Mullins rescued them both. If Mrs Clemens says we can trust him, I'd trust him with anything."

"You think very highly of Mrs Clemens," I observed.

"She's a saint," said the girl, with a blush, "Everybody knows it. She is so wonderfully kind. She taught me everything I needed to know about how to maintain this house in all its glory, down to even mixing up the simplest cleaning solution: water, vinegar and lemon juice. She also said not to mix that with another ingredient. It's one commonly used to remove difficult stains and smudges, but I can never remember its name. She never keeps it in the house for fear the children would get into it. It's outside in the storage shed."

What household liquid should the maid not mix with the cleaning solution?

"Venture a guess to this mystery ingredient, Watson?"

"Why, any sort of *eau de Javel* or bleach, I would imagine. It would create chlorine gas, which is highly toxic!"

"Very good, Watson." Turning back to the maid, he said, "Did you notice anything unusual in Mullins's behaviour since the collectors' appearance?"

"Not visibly, no. He was sometimes drunk and often

quarrelling with someone or another. He was always so, I am afraid. Like I said, he was quite different with the children: kinder and friendlier."

"Can you account for these different character aspects?"

She hesitated, before replying, "Some evenings, after supper, he spoke of the children. I asked Mrs Clemens if he had any nieces or nephews, at least, because he was so good with them, but she knew as little about his family as I did. We dared not ask him directly."

"Spot, the dog, did not take to him?"

"That's true. He is a very well-mannered dog. Spot runs to the door with his tail wagging to greet our postman, begging for treats while the postman delivers the mail and chats with Mrs Clemens. But according to our butler, Mullins smacked Spot when he was just a small puppy, for nipping Charlie while playing. The poor pup didn't know any better but has never seemed to forget the ill-treatment."

"What did you mean when you said that Mullins didn't 'visibly' change?"

"About ten days ago, Mullins decided, rather abruptly, to leave his position, an excellent one. In this economy, it was unlikely that he would quickly find another one as good in a pinch. The Bracewells pay handsomely, which is the reason why I left my long-term position with another family when I heard there was an opening here."

"What do you think drove him away? Creditors? Mrs Clemens?"

"I don't think so. If anything, Mullins would have been more likely to repay his debt with this job. He told the master that he wished to care for his parents, but he had never spoken

of them to us before."

"Did he typically get a lot of mail?"

"Not normally. But now that you mention it, he did receive a letter just before he resigned. I can't tell you anything about it because I only saw it for a moment. It was covered with strange symbols that looked like mathematics. It arrived during breakfast one morning, when our usual cook was ill, and we had the undercook make the breakfast. She swooned whenever Mullins was near the kitchen and the cook would always set her back to her tasks.

"But I digress. I remember just a quick sight of it knocking the wind out of him. He was cutting his blood sausage – I don't care for it – into slices when the letter came. He dropped his toast butter-side down in his haste to open it. Afterwards, he took a sip from the honey jar instead of his coffee mug; and he went on to spread jam over his hardboiled egg instead of eating it with the tomatoes and mushrooms. I remember that breakfast well: we teased Mullins about his having a ladylove on the sly... although one who couldn't fix him a 'proper breakfast'. The undercook blushed and left the room while Mullins focused on the letter."

For what two reasons did the undercook blush and leave the room?

"Well, you can't fault the poor woman for having an infatuation and being teased for giving Mullins an extra-special breakfast," I said. "It's more of a crime that she served a hardboiled egg with a full English breakfast rather than a fried egg!"

"Watson, stay focused," said Holmes. "Could the letter have

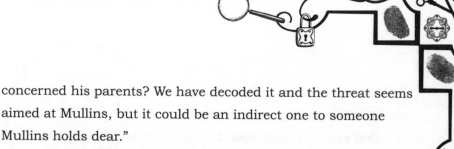

concerned his parents? We have decoded it and the threat seems aimed at Mullins, but it could be an indirect one to someone Mullins holds dear."

"At first, I thought so too, but it seems unlikely. The letter was delivered by hand, but the old butler told us that the messenger hastened away before he could speak to him. Mullins himself kept its contents a secret. From that point, I had limited contact with Mullins. That is about all I can tell you."

Before she left us, the maid turned to me and wondered, "How would you describe me in your story?"

My face flushed crimson.

"I haven't committed to writing this story yet," I replied.

"But clearly we need a report on the goings-on," she said. "Could you make me a central character? Perhaps a sidekick or a villain. Someone interesting."

I promised that I would do my best, but it doesn't do to rush into writing when the story is still unfolding.

Left alone, Holmes and I smoked our pipes in silence. I could see that his thoughts were drifting and that he was going over everything we had seen and heard today. Baker Street and all it stood for seemed awfully far away despite the comfort of our environs. I missed the noise of central London and Mrs Hudson's mixture of awe and remonstrance regarding her lodger. I felt resolved to hold Holmes to his promise.

"The scene of action reveals and confirms much of what I had suspected. I should stress, though, we have yet to interview Miss Forman, and doubtless she can tell us even more."

"Surely, Holmes, there was nothing left to be found at the crime scene. The recent rainfall will have washed away the evidence."

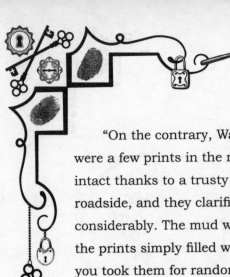

"On the contrary, Watson, there were a few prints in the mud, kept intact thanks to a trusty tree by the roadside, and they clarified matters considerably. The mud was so thick that the prints simply filled with water. Doubtless, you took them for random puddles.

"As I noted, Miss Forman's and the culprit's prints were clearly discernible. Miss Forman goes up to the driver's seat. We don't know what she sees, but she returns to the carriage, corroborating Hewitt's story."

"What about the culprit?" I asked.

"He, at some point, carried Mullins's corpse to the carriage, you see. Mullins must have been killed some time before. For now, I can't think why."

"But the gunshot was heard by both Miss Forman and Hewitt!" I exclaimed.

"A sound that resembled a gunshot was heard, but could they have distinguished a real gunshot from one like it? Whatever made the sound did not kill Mullins. Even if traces of gunpowder were washed away by the rain, there was no casing found at the crime scene.

"There's more: either Mullins or the culprit left behind a scratch on the woodwork from shoulder to waist high on the carriage as the corpse was being moved. This mark was only partially covered by the mud and appeared to begin almost where the driver's seat was located. I took a very close look at it while examining the carriage and found that it was a dull, wide mark, as opposed to a deep, narrow cut that is wider and deeper at the top and then becomes shallower towards its other end. It is extremely likely that it was manmade rather than made by something brushing into the carriage. What does this tell you, Watson?"

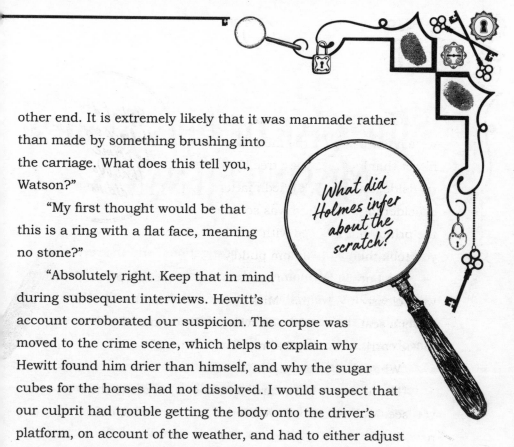

What did Holmes infer about the scratch?

"My first thought would be that this is a ring with a flat face, meaning no stone?"

"Absolutely right. Keep that in mind during subsequent interviews. Hewitt's account corroborated our suspicion. The corpse was moved to the crime scene, which helps to explain why Hewitt found him drier than himself, and why the sugar cubes for the horses had not dissolved. I would suspect that our culprit had trouble getting the body onto the driver's platform, on account of the weather, and had to either adjust his grip or pick him up once again."

"What do we know about the culprit?" I repeated.

"Our man is tall, rather more than six feet. One ought to make a study of footprints and strides to be a model investigator, Watson. He shares your tastes in cigars. The stub he left was from a Bolivar."

"But Holmes," I said, "Bracewell, Hewitt, Mullins and even you fit that description; and Bracewell, Hewitt and Mullins wore rings!"

"My dear Watson, you are learning! None of us is above suspicion, not even myself."

Now turn to page 132.

THE CASE OF MRS KEMP'S MISSING TENANTS

After almost two days of investigations, and the revelation that Miss Forman was the daughter of the dearly departed Harry Mullins, we wished to speak with her directly. Not only about the crimes committed, but to also determine any involvement she may have had.

As we were leaving the cottage in Kent, one of Holmes's urchins came up to us and bowed deeply. He gave Holmes a telegram, which he tore open.

"Our nets are ready, my dear Watson. We shall catch our museum culprit before too long. He is a clever man all right, but he is scared."

"Scared?" I wondered aloud. "He's killed at least one man."

"Yes, but all is not as it seems, Watson. The most dangerous force behind this mystery is one that we cannot see."

Holmes withdrew his pocketbook, scribbled a quick note in pencil and tore out the page. He gave it to the young boy, along with a sovereign: "Make sure that this goes to Mrs Hudson and no one else. Make sure you stay outside when you deliver it to her and do not antagonise her while you are there, or I shall find others to deliver my messages." The boy scowled but gave another bow and ran in the opposite direction.

We boarded the train back to London and continued our journey to Mrs Kemp's boarding house.

As we travelled through the countryside, I pressed Holmes

for answers – why all the telegrams? – but I received no reply. His demeanour showed that he knew more than he would say, but I could make neither head nor tail of what was going on. It need not follow, as Holmes surmised, that Miss Forman murdered her father, even if she had known that he was driving the cab. And yet, she was at the scene of the crime. Although a detective ought to be impartial, I wished very much that Miss Forman would prove innocent.

As we neared London the train was delayed at a danger signal. But we then left the station after Holmes bought a newspaper. We took a cab to take us through the city to the north. Holmes looked out of the window, pointing out different landmarks noteworthy only to him. He became somewhat lost in thought as we passed a row of smart townhouses on Upper Wimpole Street in Marylebone. Number two seemed to pique his interest. He smiled to himself, shook his head slightly and went on reading his newspaper.

What is it about this address that distracts Holmes?

As I sat next to him, I read the headlines of the newspaper he was holding up. I could see nothing about the murder of Mullins or the missing Bracewell children. Lestrade and Gregson were doing a good job of keeping these crimes out of the press. After he had held his newspaper for a while unread, I eventually asked my companion why he was lost in thought. He replied that an up-and-coming writer had garnered his interest and he believed him to have a long and eventful career in prospect.

We made it from the railway station to the London Underground, then travelled back to Finchley, whereupon we took a cab to Mrs Kemp's address.

As we approached the house, we found Mrs Kemp hard at work in her garden, which started at the front and carried on around the side of the house to the back. She waved to us with her trowel and beckoned us towards her. Holmes and I wove around the intricate pathway trying to avoid the piles of mud, but to no avail. The plants were thriving after the rains of the past week. As we reached her, we complimented Mrs Kemp on her skills at maintaining such a varied garden. For my part, I could not determine all the species of plants here. Some I knew from my medical textbooks, and it was clear that Mrs Kemp was not motivated solely by aesthetic value. Holmes stopped at different locations, studying a few choice species and the layout of the garden.

"You are hard at work, Mrs Kemp," said Holmes. "Your garden is lovely."

"It is hard work, Mr Holmes, but I grow a lot of my own food and medicinal herbs, as well as flowers," said Mrs Kemp. "It is only over the last year that the garden has become so magnificent. I've been working for most of the afternoon. Your visit is timely, as I was about to take a break. Would you both care for some tea?"

"A spot of refreshment would be much appreciated," I said.

"Have you made any new discoveries?" Mrs Kemp inquired, as we wound our way back along the path and towards the front door.

"Not one," Holmes replied swiftly, giving me a look that said to keep the results of our investigation to ourselves. "We wondered if we might speak with Miss Forman again. Perhaps she is feeling better than she did this morning."

"I dare say she is. She has been resting since you left and I

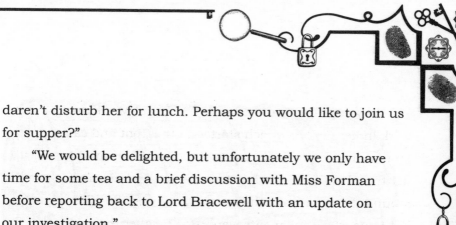

daren't disturb her for lunch. Perhaps you would like to join us for supper?"

"We would be delighted, but unfortunately we only have time for some tea and a brief discussion with Miss Forman before reporting back to Lord Bracewell with an update on our investigation."

"Oh yes, the poor man," she said, ushering us into the boarding house. We painstakingly scraped off as much mud as we could from our clothes before entering. We sat down on a sofa in the small sitting room, next to a window that overlooked the garden. Holmes moved a golden candlestick of Psyche to a different table so as to not block the view. He examined it for a moment and we both saw the engraving on the underside: "To my Love".

Mrs Kemp asked a maid to make some tea and to seek out Miss Forman before going upstairs to change out of her muddy boots and gloves. Holmes and I were directed to a larger living room. As with the building's exterior, there was no discernible unifying theme: a medieval helmet stood on a mantelpiece beside a Grecian urn. None of the items of furniture matched any of the others, but the result was oddly comforting. Holmes sat on an ottoman, which enabled me, when I sat on a higher chair, to look him in the eye. He struggled to get comfortable on it, and as he manoeuvred himself, we heard a noise from beneath him.

He opened the lid of the ottoman. A small box sat inside with another engraving that read "To my Love". There was a picture of a single arrow shooting through a heart. On the front of the box was a lock that had five dials, each of which showed a different series of letters. My friend opened it in mere seconds.

How did Holmes unlock the box?

"What have you there, Holmes, and how on Earth did you open it so quickly?" I asked.

"It appears to be a pair of spectacles. Judging by the style, I would say they belong to a male. One with very poor eyesight, judging by the lenses. And, since you ask, to open the box I simply thought back to the engraving on the candlestick of Psyche. That too read, 'To my Love'. Psyche's partner was Cupid, and this was the five-letter word that unlocked the box." Holmes replaced the spectacles in the box and once again attempted a position of comfort on the ottoman.

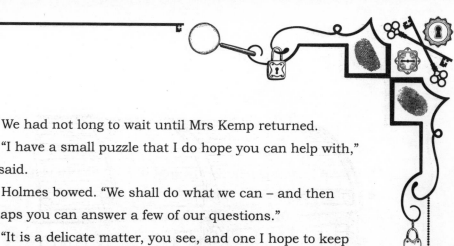

We had not long to wait until Mrs Kemp returned.

"I have a small puzzle that I do hope you can help with," she said.

Holmes bowed. "We shall do what we can – and then perhaps you can answer a few of our questions."

"It is a delicate matter, you see, and one I hope to keep private." Here, she glanced my way, but my friend would have none of it:

"Whatever you have to say can be said before Dr Watson."

"Very well. It is this: about three months ago, a man asked if he could occupy a flat in this house. There's nothing unusual in that: it is a spacious quarter and some tenants hope for privacy, for which the apartment, being so removed, would be ideal. The place is unfurnished, and the tenant offered a very generous sum; one that could finance the completion of the renovations that were underway at the time. I agreed immediately, before leaving town for a few weeks to help my ailing mother. Ordinarily, I rent only to female tenants, but all of my rooms were unoccupied at the time, so I decided it would be better to accept the income that would help me finish my renovations and deal with any other problems later.

"I left my maid to see to the new tenant's needs and ensure that the builders arrived each day to work on the renovations. On my return, the maid confessed that she had only seen the new tenant on the day he moved in. He paid the workers to help him carry a large trunk and a few items of furniture to his room."

"Nothing you've mentioned so far seems out of the ordinary, despite your decision to rent to a man, which is not the normal profile of boarders in your house," said Holmes. "What seems to be the matter?"

"The tenant caused no trouble, mind you, but therein the confusion lies: I have seen no one come in or go out. The bills have been promptly paid on the first of each month by post, and no further request of any kind has been made. For all intents and purposes, the flat seemed vacant, but the money kept coming in, so that is why I have not felt guilty about renting my other rooms as the need arose, despite there being a man in an otherwise all-female boarding house."

"Are you entirely sure that the flat has been empty all this time?" I asked.

"As I said, I have seen no one come in or go out. The front and back doors are the only points of entry and the room has been locked from the inside ever since."

"Have you heard sounds from the room?" asked Holmes.

"None whatsoever."

"Can you describe the person who approached you?"

"The meeting was brief, and his every question and response were matter-of-fact. His moustache was rather spectacular, as was his beard. He had a twinkle in his eye." Mrs Kemp then said more quietly, leaning forward: "Between you and me, I thought he took a liking to me."

"I am sure his facial hair, in all its prominence, was fake," said Holmes. "Did you notice anything else? Did he speak about himself at all?"

"He was a medium-built man, rather shorter than Dr Watson. He said little besides how much he values privacy."

"Then I must congratulate you on finding an ideal tenant."

"Far from it. I have never seen him since."

Holmes stroked his chin and asked at last: "Can we see the flat?"

What is unusual about this room?

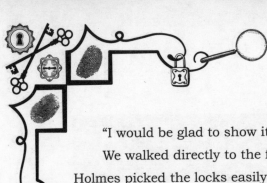

"I would be glad to show it to you," Mrs Kemp said.

We walked directly to the flat, to a double-locked door. Holmes picked the locks easily and entered the room. A window with a frame that had been painted shut overlooked the gardens far below. I looked outside and noticed that it was a far drop to the ground. There was no way to climb down or up without risk of serious injury. Next to the window stood a large empty bookcase. A small bed sat along the opposite wall; it had a pillow but no sheets, and a table next to it. A large, unlocked trunk stood open at the foot of the bed. The flowered wallpaper looked new. I commented on it to Mrs Kemp.

"Oh, yes," she replied. "I had the workmen install this before the tenant moved in. It is modelled after one of the flowers in my garden. I did not know if the room would be too feminine for my unseen tenant, but he took it nonetheless. Mr Holmes, do you have any insights into the nature of the unseen man?"

"There is something unusual about this room," said Holmes.

"You say that you haven't seen the tenant come or go, no sound has been heard and the door has been locked for the three months you've rented it," said Holmes.

"Yes," confirmed Mrs Kemp. "I've given you all the information I have about this mysterious man."

"The window is painted shut so does not function as a point of entrance or departure. But if you look at the wallpaper, the pattern is somewhat disrupted next to the bookcase."

Holmes walked over to the area he indicated and ran his hand along the pattern. He pulled out a small penknife, slid it in next to the wallpaper and pulled. To our astonishment, a small door opened in the wall. Behind it was a space that included another window. This one opened onto the roof.

"This is how your tenant has been getting in and out," explained Holmes.

"This wasn't here before!" exclaimed Mrs Kemp. "I would have known about it. How did it get here? And when?"

"The obvious answer is that your tenant paid your workers to have this installed while you were away," said Holmes. "He likely offered them a hefty sum to conceal the door in the wall, include a new window and keep it from you. The window is not visible from the ground, so you wouldn't have noticed it. The question now is why did he go to these lengths?"

At that moment, the maid appeared: "Mrs Kemp, I'm afraid Miss Forman has gone missing!" My friend did not seem surprised and he shared none of Mrs Kemp's anxiety. The gentlewoman dashed across the house to another room. We followed a short distance behind. Inside the room, we saw a bed with a note on the pillow in a strange hand, a desk, a large wardrobe with a few items of clothing and a mirror on the inside door. Holmes crossed the room to the open window. I followed him. Beneath the window was a collection of ladders.

About three feet beneath the window was a large, wooden trellis running from the ground almost to the base of this second-storey window. To the right of where we stood was a large tree, with an extremely long, thick branch running parallel to the house. A tall ladder was propped up against it. Furthermore, two smaller ladders were propped up against the house about a yard away from the left of the window. The grounds themselves were excellently kept and there was a neat design to the layout of all the plants in the garden.

How did Miss Forman escape from this room?

"It is clear that Miss Forman escaped via this window shortly after we left the house earlier today. There are two ways she could have reached the ground from here. She could have lowered herself from the window, getting a foothold on the trellis and climbing down. Or, if she is an adventurous soul, she could have jumped from the window onto the branch, crawled to the trunk and asked for a gardener to help her down with a ladder.

"She must have changed her clothes," Holmes continued. "Were there any men's clothes in the wardrobe?"

"Why, yes, as it happens. An actress lodged here some months ago and she left behind some of her belongings. I didn't move them, in case they could be of use to others. Why would Miss Forman leave in such a manner?" Mrs Kemp wondered.

Holmes looked pointedly at Mrs Kemp and said: "Dear woman, it is time for you to stop your deceit. You knew that Miss Forman left your abode soon after Watson and I departed, and you have been serving as an alibi since we arrived this afternoon. What is your involvement in the events that have transpired?"

"Mr Holmes!" gasped Mrs Kemp, "Whatever do you mean? I have only tried to help the poor woman ever since she was brought to me."

"That is one thing I am struggling to understand," said Holmes. "Why was Miss Forman brought to you rather than taken to a doctor or a hospital? Mr Hewitt must have brought her here for a reason, or did she orchestrate her own arrival?"

"I'd never met Miss Forman before she was brought here by Mr Hewitt," said Mrs Kemp, "And I only know George Hewitt in passing. He is our postman."

"You are lying about at least one of those statements."

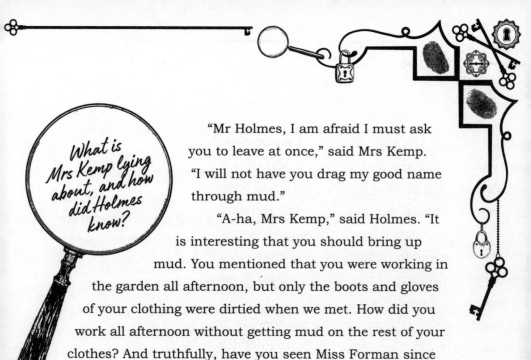

What is Mrs Kemp lying about, and how did Holmes know?

"Mr Holmes, I am afraid I must ask you to leave at once," said Mrs Kemp. "I will not have you drag my good name through mud."

"A-ha, Mrs Kemp," said Holmes. "It is interesting that you should bring up mud. You mentioned that you were working in the garden all afternoon, but only the boots and gloves of your clothing were dirtied when we met. How did you work all afternoon without getting mud on the rest of your clothes? And truthfully, have you seen Miss Forman since our departure earlier today?"

"I have not seen Miss Forman since this morning," Mrs Kemp said sternly. "If muddy boots and gloves are all you have to go on, I suggest you call the constable and tell him this tale. We shall see what he has to say."

"Very well then." Holmes appeared to accept that Mrs Kemp hadn't aided Amelia's escape. He looked her square in the eye. "What is your relationship with George Hewitt?"

Mrs Kemp blanched, and answered with a slight tremble in her voice: "I have seen him in the neighbourhood. That is all."

"There are a few pieces of evidence that convince me otherwise," said Holmes.

"Holmes, whatever do you mean?" I asked.

"Watson, Mrs Kemp and Mr Hewitt are more involved with each other than either of them wishes to divulge. The first piece of evidence is this: they share a pair of matching gold candlesticks. Hewitt has Cupid; Mrs Kemp has Psyche. According to the Greek myth, Cupid and Psyche were lovers, so it would make sense that a pair of lovers would keep one each."

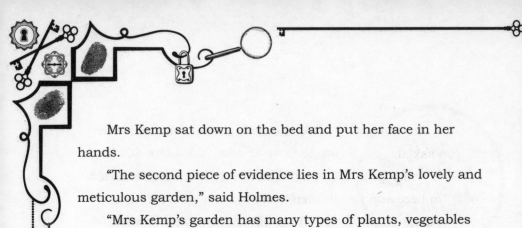

Mrs Kemp sat down on the bed and put her face in her hands.

"The second piece of evidence lies in Mrs Kemp's lovely and meticulous garden," said Holmes.

"Mrs Kemp's garden has many types of plants, vegetables and flowers," I said. "I don't see what any of them have to do with the postman."

"It is not what lies within the garden," said Holmes. "It is how it is laid out. Mrs Kemp prides herself on her gardening skills. If you look at the garden from the window, there is a curious pattern to it that I could not see from the ground. Viewed from above, the pattern comes into focus."

What is it about Mrs Kemp's garden that links her to George Hewitt?

I walked to the window and looked again at the garden to the side of the house. After a few moments, I saw what Holmes was referring to.

"The plants here are planted in a pattern where a 'K' and an 'H' overlap," I said with awe. "Kemp and Hewitt... their initials are intertwined. And in a garden, a thing of beauty where new life grows. How fitting."

"And finally, we found a pair of spectacles in the ottoman. Hewitt told Lestrade and us that he had misplaced his spectacles a few days before he came upon the Bracewell carriage. Are those not George Hewitt's glasses, madame?" Holmes asked.

Mrs Kemp began sobbing. "You are right, Mr Holmes. He left them here and I have been keeping them safe. I have not been forthcoming with you, but I will not say another word."

"Perhaps we should direct our attention to the note on Miss Forman's pillow," said Holmes. He walked over and picked it up. "This ought to give us answers about her involvement or reveal what she has discovered for herself about the crimes so far."

Holmes studied the note and the curious writing:

> To Detective Sherlock Holmes and Dr John Watson:
> I leave this, my sworn statement, as to the true events
> of my involvement with the mystery surrounding the
> Bracewell driver and my missing charges.

"What do you make of it?" I asked.

"Is it not obvious, Watson?" Holmes replied.

"It doesn't look like English or any other language I've seen," I said.

"It is English," corrected Holmes. "You are not looking at it properly, though."

What has Holmes deciphered about the mysterious note?

With that, he picked up the note and walked to the wardrobe, opened the door and held the note in front of the mirror. I stood next to him and looked at the paper.

I could now read what Miss Forman had written.

"Miss Forman has left us her statement," said Holmes,

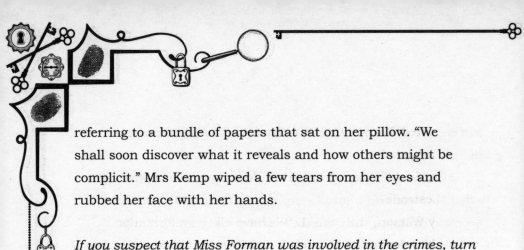

referring to a bundle of papers that sat on her pillow. "We shall soon discover what it reveals and how others might be complicit." Mrs Kemp wiped a few tears from her eyes and rubbed her face with her hands.

If you suspect that Miss Forman was involved in the crimes, turn to page 161.

If you suspect that Miss Forman is innocent, turn to page 184.

We exited 221B Baker Street to find a vacant cab parked not far from our home.

"What luck!" I exclaimed. "How do you know where we are to meet Lestrade?"

"Why Watson," he replied. "We have all the information we need in the telegram. Did you not deduce where in Finchley our meeting with Lestrade is to take place?"

I confessed that the message was mysterious to my untrained eyes.

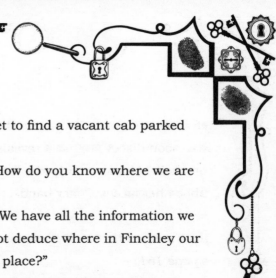

Where in town are they to meet Lestrade?

"The telegram is as cryptic regarding the precise location where we are to meet him as it is in pinpointing Finchley. The location resides in the rest of the telegram. 'Heavy is the head that wears the crown' is an echo of Shakespeare's Henry IV, part 2: 'Uneasy lies the head that wears a crown.' The head that is heavy is the king's head, and we are to meet Lestrade for a drink at the King's Head pub, a stone's throw away from the railway station.'

Holmes announced our destination and the driver immediately whipped his horses to a gallop. But a gallop was not to be had, for the horses and the wheels of the cab frequently stuck in the mud. Travel was slow going. More infuriating still was the addition of another passenger soon after we embarked, which also prevented me from asking Holmes more questions.

With the weight of an additional man, one of the rear wheels finally got trapped in the mud. Try as he might, the driver could not get the horses to move another inch. The other passenger and I, along with the driver, got out to push the cab

as Holmes commanded the horses. Eventually we were moving once more. This procedure was to repeat itself many more times along the journey, even long after our fellow passenger disembarked in Golders Green. Holmes, for his part, managed to keep his coat remarkably clean, and seemed to enjoy the trip immensely. I tried to kick the mud off my boots and pants, but to little avail.

The routine caused us, or at least me, to lose our sense of time and place. The rocking of the carriage had a soothing effect after our exertions. At length, we found ourselves admiring St Michael's Church, which towered over us. Suddenly, Holmes lurched out of his seat.

"Driver!" Holmes cried. "Stop this cab immediately!"

The driver pretended not to hear until Holmes began rapping on the window. Fearing that he would shatter it entirely, the driver, at last, pulled the cab to a stop.

Why did Holmes stop the cab?

"Surely," Holmes said, "you know that we are going in the wrong direction. We are in Highgate, which is far to the south and east from Finchley!"

The man, sufficiently cowed, admitted, "I meant no harm. I was given a half-sovereign by the fare before you and instructed to wait outside your flat. I was promised a second half-sovereign to delay you thus by going through the muddiest streets, and a third to pick him up again not far from where you hailed me."

"I will give you a fourth half-sovereign if you can describe this man."

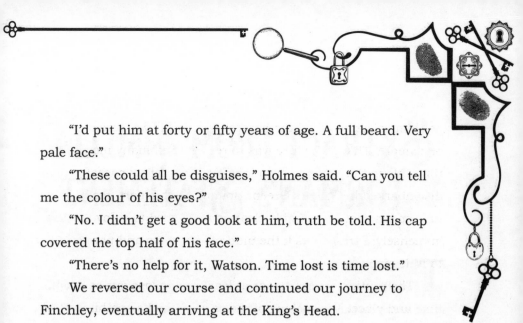

"I'd put him at forty or fifty years of age. A full beard. Very pale face."

"These could all be disguises," Holmes said. "Can you tell me the colour of his eyes?"

"No. I didn't get a good look at him, truth be told. His cap covered the top half of his face."

"There's no help for it, Watson. Time lost is time lost."

We reversed our course and continued our journey to Finchley, eventually arriving at the King's Head.

Now turn to page 86.

EXTRACT FROM AMELIA FORMAN'S STATEMENT

Thus far, I have pieced together the story from my recollections – with the occasional nudge from Holmes, who is far more forthcoming with criticism than with praise – and from sources such as telegrams, newspapers and diaries. The time is ripe, however, to hand over this narrative entirely to a different storyteller and it will imminently become apparent why.

My Statement: Amelia Forman, ▓▓▓▓▓▓▓

I have been asked to relay my version of events and my part in this story, at the direction of Mr Holmes and a man introduced to me as Inspector Lestrade. I shall account for my time since Mr Sherlock Holmes and Dr Watson visited Mrs Kemp. However, my statement would benefit from starting a little before that.

It is certainly true that when I awoke to find myself in my esteemed caregiver's home, I was quite unwell, but I was stronger than she took me for. I am no detective, but I am – and always have been – an avid reader, especially of mysteries. I have revisited the

What is the date of the statement?

events of that day many a time in the solitude of my
bedroom, which smelled slightly of cabbage — there is
no other way to describe it, as much as I admire Mrs
Kemp. I could not help but ponder over the mysteries:
who had killed the coachman? Why was he dry? Were
the children trying to tell us something when they left
a bookmark at the map in Treasure Island? Everyone
knows that the map does little to advance the plot.
And most curiously, where are the children now?

To be entirely frank, I didn't have a huge amount
of faith in the detective and his companion when we
first met. Mr Holmes stared at me rather blankly
while Dr Watson gave me a medical examination.
Aside from his role as a doctor, he seemed little help
to Holmes at all. Upon completion of Dr Watson's
examination, Mr Holmes asked the most mundane
questions. I failed to see how they were relevant.
My answers left Holmes looking bored and Watson
seemingly puzzled.

Shortly after they left, I decided to take matters
into my own hands. I told Mrs Kemp that I wanted to
write a note to thank George Hewitt for bringing me
to her. She provided me with a pen, paper and his
address. She knew the address by heart, which struck
me as odd considering that they have only a passing
acquaintance. I promptly discharged a note before
explaining to my hostess that I felt exhausted from the
morning's labour. From there, I could set the next part
of my plan into action.

Mrs Kemp offered to send for a doctor, but I
would hear none of it. I was fit as a fiddle and eager
to inspect my surroundings. I locked the door behind

me and looked into the wardrobe where I found some walking clothes. Male costume is not foreign to me: I regularly wore items from my stepfather's wardrobe when my siblings and I staged home theatricals.

The maid was working downstairs and Mrs Kemp was reading in the living room, so there was no way for me to exit in my disguise without being noticed. I looked out of the window. There was scaffolding outside and I had my choice of two or three ladders. It was an easy escape route indeed. I watched as Holmes and Watson walked away ever so slowly. Mr Holmes seemed to keep pontificating to the good doctor in his booming voice, who - to my ears and eyes - provided nary a response by voice or gesture. Finally, when the coast was clear, I climbed out of the window, arranged my footing on one of the ladders below and made my way down to the lawn. I followed the pair from a safe distance in my new clothes.

I overheard Holmes saying to Watson that they were headed to Cromwell's. I wondered why. There was nothing the employment agency could tell them that I hadn't reported in my diary. By now, I'm sure you will have ascertained that I don't hold the detective in very high regard.

For want of 'leads', as they call them, I followed Holmes and Watson to London's West End. I was surprised to see so much commotion in front of Cromwell's. True, there is always traffic in this part of town, but rarely a crowd outside the employment agency. Policemen, newsies and curious onlookers all clamoured to be heard.

I stopped one passer-by and asked him what the matter was.

"There was a break-in," he said.

"A break-in?" I repeated in astonishment.

"That's what I said," and with that he glowered at me, as though I was accusing him of falsehood.

"Was anyone hurt?" I continued.

"I hear there was a murder!" he exclaimed.

"Two," said the young boy standing next to him.

"Arson, they say," argued a woman, holding the boy's hand.

"Vandalism," disagreed an old man standing nearby.

It was impossible to sort out the facts from the fibs. Each spectator had his or her own interpretation of events. I strode up to a policeman on duty and pulled out a spare piece of paper I had got from Mrs Kemp and a pen. I could see he was about to order me back with the rest of the crowd, when I spoke to him in a low gruff voice.

Knowing that the peeler wouldn't reveal information to any old person about whatever crime had been committed, I identified myself as a member of the press and asked what had transpired. He looked around quickly, I assume to see if a supervisor was present, and then asked me not to include his name, before telling me the clean, straight facts of the case. There were not many: Cromwell's was broken into and some records were stolen.

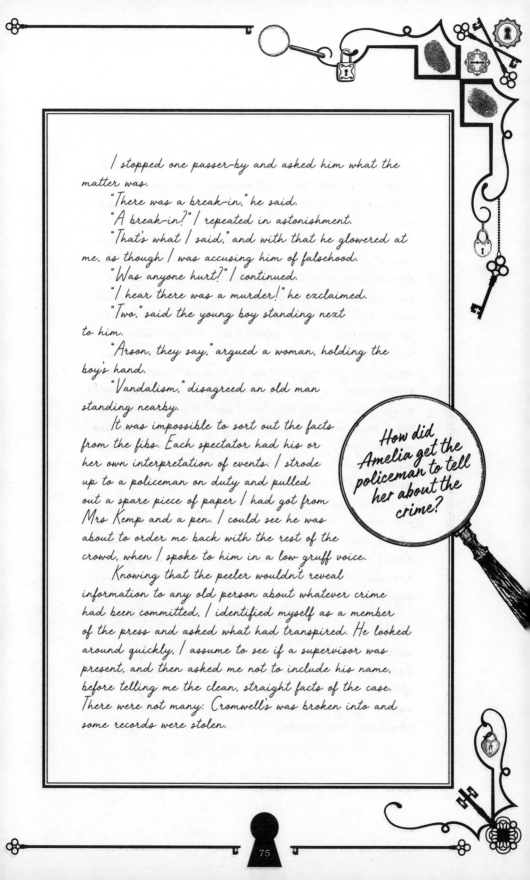

How did Amelia get the policeman to tell her about the crime?

I knew better than to keep following Holmes and Watson. I thought Mr Holmes must have been following a tangent to the main mystery, and I decided to stick to the matter at hand. An idea began to form in my mind. I would talk to Mr Hewitt the postman, find out the facts of this case myself and thereby solve the mystery before the famous detective.

I concealed my face with a cap as I walked past them, and they noticed not a thing. While a policeman led away Miss Stoper, and others in the crowd questioned anyone in sight, I smiled: Miss Stoper was finally getting her comeuppance. After seeing my potential salary at the Bracewells she had spoken to me in a way I did not care for. I stole away and made for Mr Hewitt's address. I was going to take matters into my own hands.

Let me explain my reasoning. From the first, I knew that there was something mysterious about the circumstances of my employment. The pay was too generous for the services I could offer, and furthermore, I had no interview with my employer nor with a person from his household.

As mysterious as such circumstances were, they did not seem related to the children's disappearance. I may have been hired hastily, but it need not follow that I was hired to enable the kidnapping of the children, with the crime blamed partly on me. I now cared less about discovering why I was employed than I did for the children's recovery. The missing link, I suspected, lay with George Hewitt. I was frightened to visit him, make no mistake; a man had already been

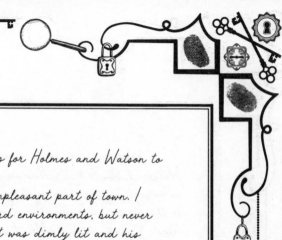

killed. It would take hours for Holmes and Watson to
catch up, if they ever did.

George lived in an unpleasant part of town. I
have spent time in untoward environments, but never
one such as this. The street was dimly lit and his
door was at the end of a dark alley. I wished I had
company, for I was afraid not only of the stray dogs
and rats but also of what I was about to do. I walked
around the house, surveying its layout, and jumped as
I heard a dog howl nearby. I eventually found the back
of the house, which I describe here:

I saw a laundress labouring over a washtub in
a small yard next-door to Hewitt's house. To steel my
nerves and give myself time, I struck up a conversation.

"Excuse me," I asked, deepening my tone to the best
male voice I could muster, to match my clothes, "Can
you tell me where I can find Mr George Hewitt?"

"H'witt, ya want? He lives there. Yer practically
standin' in his yard," she said, eyeing me suspiciously
before pointing at the house: "Wha' d'ya want 'im fer?"

"He's my uncle," I said.

"I never 'eard 'im talk about a nephew."

"We were never close."

"That explains it," she replied. She returned to her
scrubbing, but then added: "He wasn't always like this,
ya know."

"Like what?"

"Broken. He was hon'rable, see. Ya should know
that about 'im before ya see 'im. He's not likely to be as
ya or yer family would remember."

"How is he now?" I asked.

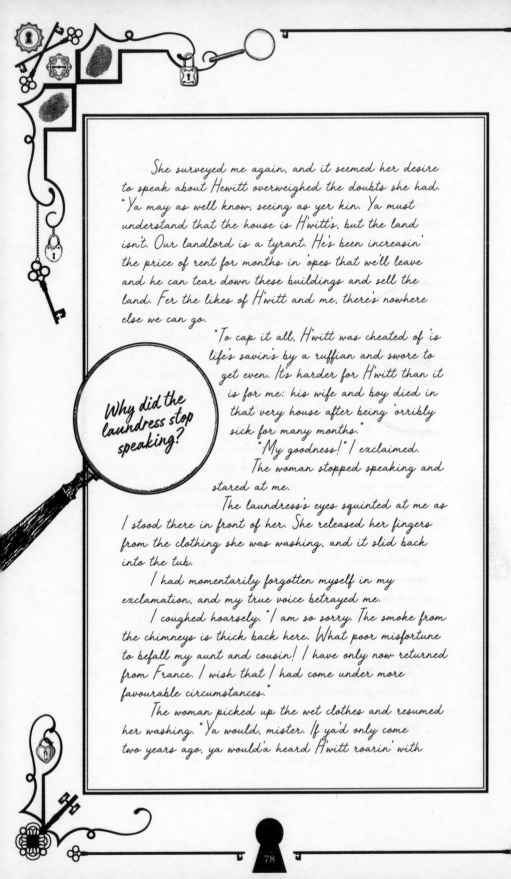

She surveyed me again, and it seemed her desire to speak about Hewitt overweighed the doubts she had. "Ya may as well know, seeing as yer kin. Ya must understand that the house is H'witt's, but the land isn't. Our landlord is a tyrant. He's been increasin' the price of rent for months in 'opes that we'll leave and he can tear down these buildings and sell the land. Fer the likes of H'witt and me, there's nowhere else we can go.

"To cap it all, H'witt was cheated of 'is life's savin's by a ruffian and swore to get even. It's harder for H'witt than it is for me: his wife and boy died in that very house after being 'orribly sick for many months."

"My goodness!" I exclaimed.

The woman stopped speaking and stared at me.

The laundress's eyes squinted at me as I stood there in front of her. She released her fingers from the clothing she was washing, and it slid back into the tub.

I had momentarily forgotten myself in my exclamation, and my true voice betrayed me.

I coughed hoarsely. "I am so sorry. The smoke from the chimneys is thick back here. What poor misfortune to befall my aunt and cousin! I have only now returned from France. I wish that I had come under more favourable circumstances."

The woman picked up the wet clothes and resumed her washing. "Ya would, mister. If ya'd only come two years ago, ya would'a heard H'witt roarin' with

Why did the laundress stop speaking?

laughter and his son balancing hisself on 'is shoulders. Now he runs 'imself ragged with extra shifts and post routes ta pay back his mountin' debts. I 'eard he's been tryin' to increase his savings by playin' games of chance with local scoundrels."

I bit my lip to stifle a sob. I didn't want to give away my disguise. "Is there no hope for him?"

"None. Bracewell, the devil! I spit at his name! He and 'is 'enchman would have us out one way or another. It is not long now before we will all b'gone. You'd better go in. H'witt will be leaving for his shift ere long."

A-ha, I thought to myself. The final pieces of the puzzle have clicked into place. If my suspicions are correct, I will have bested the famous Sherlock Holmes! But, poor, poor Mr Hewitt.

I thanked the laundress and made my way to the front door. I raised my hand to knock just as it was opening and came face to face with Hewitt. His expression was one of sorrow, despair and fear. My countenance softened at knowing his misfortune and my eyes moistened with tears. I feared that could be my cover blown, as he scrutinised me, recognition dawning in his red-rimmed eyes:

"What do you want, ma'am?"

With my ruse discovered, I abandoned my disguise.

"I've come to warn you," I muttered softly.

At this, it was Hewitt's turn to be surprised. He

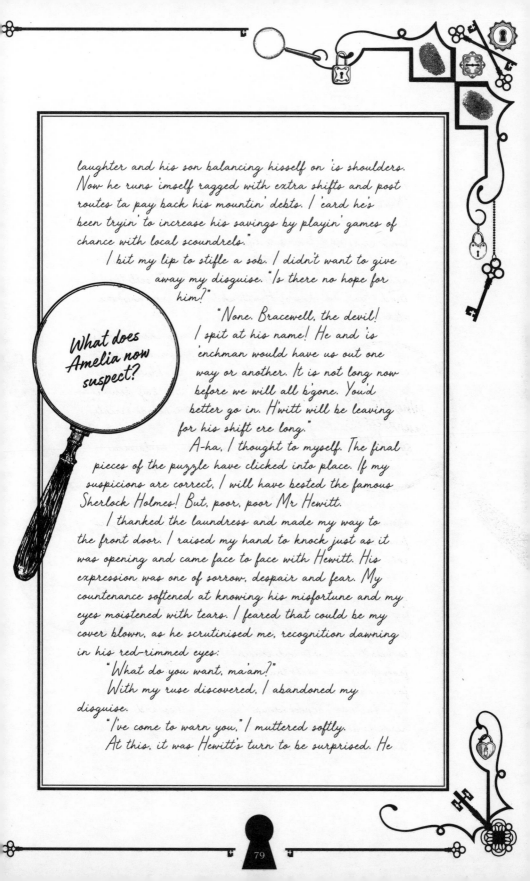

What does Amelia now suspect?

led me into the house and motioned to some overturned crates that served as his chairs. I glanced around Hewitt's home and saw a small dish of water on the floor, a ball half-hidden by one of the crates, a copy of *Treasure Island* that seemed to have been knocked to the floor and three glasses sitting near the kitchen sink.

He sat across from me.

"I did not mean for any of this to happen!" he cried, with desperation.

"But it has. You killed a man and kidnapped the children. I don't care for Bracewell's hired detective and his friend, but I fear they have figured out where the children are, which means the trouble will catch up with you. You must leave now and never return."

"It is not fair," said Mr Hewitt. His finger traced the figure of Cupid on the candlestick nearby. "I was trying to put my life back together after losing my family."

"I agree, life hasn't dealt you a fair hand, but what you did was wrong."

He paused and toyed with his hat. "Why are you helping me?" He asked.

"I work neither for the police nor for the detective. As their governess, my only concern is that the children are unharmed and I think that it's about time that you returned them to their father."

He became startled. "How do you know where they are?" he asked.

"It is apparent that they are close by," I said,

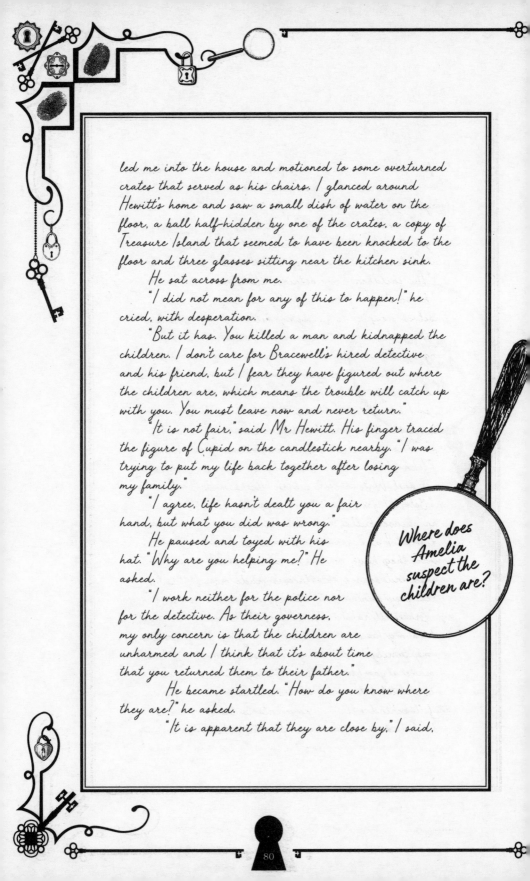

Where does Amelia suspect the children are?

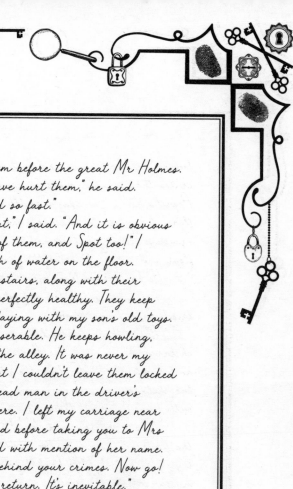

satisfied that I found them before the great Mr Holmes.

"I never would have hurt them," he said. "Everything just happened so fast."

"I understand that," I said. "And it is obvious that you took good care of them, and Spot too!" I gestured towards the dish of water on the floor.

"The children are upstairs, along with their dog," he said. "They are perfectly healthy. They keep themselves occupied by playing with my son's old toys. It is their dog who is miserable. He keeps howling, setting off the strays in the alley. It was never my intention to take them, but I couldn't leave them locked in the carriage with a dead man in the driver's seat, so I brought them here. I left my carriage near the large pond in the mud before taking you to Mrs Kemp's." His eyes glistened with mention of her name.

"I know the reason behind your crimes. Now go! Holmes and Watson will return. It's inevitable."

"Before I go, I want to clarify one matter. It is not an excuse, but it provides an explanation for why I did what I did. Mullins was as bad as his master. Together, they have robbed me of everything I own. My wife and son's long illnesses made me poor, but I ensured they wanted for nothing in their last days.

"Bracewell raised the rent of the lease of the land on which my house stood twice in a year. The expenses from my family's deaths took almost everything I had, so I made a gamble. I lost all of my savings - not knowing until later that Mullins was a cheat - and then fell behind with my payments to the Bracewells. Mullins made an offer to me for the house well below its value, knowing that I had no choice but to take it.

"I confronted Mullins about his swindling. I came upon him in an alley outside his local pub. He was drunk and became violent when I accused him. He pulled out a gun and we struggled. A shot was fired, and he collapsed. I only had moments to decide what to do, so I pushed his body into the trunk attached to my carriage and drove home. I found some pieces of torn up paper. I wanted to discover what his instructions had been, or he would have been discovered missing."

	this Saturda	nething abou	staff. It's t
u,	too. We nee		M
tion	'M' when u		
ease collect	Take the chi	t them.	ldren,
erness, from	out these visi	rs Clemens	tors from
	hey are scar		na the
Miss Forma	me to do som	Can you ple	y at noon?
Finchley Sta		the new gove	d to talk ab
			ou return. T

I stared at the slips of paper for a few seconds, and then started piecing them together. I read the message and nodded for George to continue.

"I found a paper on him with

What does the message say?

instructions for him to collect the children the next morning from the front of the house, then to take them to the railway station to pick you up at noon. I felt so guilty about what I had done that, when I found money on him, I left it in his pocket. I wore a long coat, like his, and a cap, parked my carriage near the muddy puddle that had formed over the previous week, where nobody was likely to pass, and walked the rest of the way to Westwood Manor.

"I found the key to the carriage near the stable. I hitched the horses, drove to the house where the children were waiting, then went on to the station to collect you. The route was clear, and I thought I could get away with staging his murder with a blank gunshot. I pulled his body from my carriage, near the trees, carried it to the Bracewell carriage and stowed it in the driver's seat.

"I believed I was in the clear and was about to go to the police. I never dreamed that you would come out to investigate. I hid nearby smoking my cigar when I saw you exit the carriage, examine Mullins's body and then injure yourself as you tried to go back to the carriage. I could not have another death on my hands, especially with the children around. I was left with no choice. I took the key I had given you, unlocked the carriage, placed the children in my carriage and brought them here, only a short distance away. I then returned to the carriage to bring you to Mrs Kemp's. And then finally, I reported the crime to the police.

"I was just trying to rebuild my life. If only I had told Mrs Kemp what was going on. Perhaps things

would have been different if she knew that I was losing my house..." His voice trailed off.

My sympathies were with the poor man. For all the mistakes that he had made, it was Harry Mullins who drove him to his last desperate act. He was guilty only of deception. He did not kill a man in cold blood. I made my decision quickly and repeated: "Leave now and never return." His story had taken a while to tell, and I was panicking that the detective would arrive at any minute.

He took a long look at me and began to pack his few belongings. He handed me the gold candlestick and bade me give it to Mrs Kemp. I secured it in my long coat and assured him that I would do so.

As he was about to leave, I told him to lock the door behind him. I went upstairs to check on the children and told them that they would be going home soon. I returned downstairs to the crate I had been sitting on and thought about all that had transpired.

It was not long before Holmes, Watson and two men I did not know arrived. With my disguise abandoned, I told them that the children were safe upstairs. I waited on the crate for them to confirm this fact, knowing their questioning would begin soon.

At first, Holmes was preoccupied in telling me about Lord Bracewell, who is apparently a relative pretending to be my employer. It matters little to me, since I have not met the real Lord. I could see, though, that Holmes was directing our attentions to the children upstairs, distracting us from this relative of Bracewell. We - except for Bracewell - collected the

children and Spot the dog.

When Lestrade was out of earshot, Holmes asked me to write the statement that you are reading. Perhaps, Holmes, you will think me an accessory to Hewitt's escape, but perhaps I could say the same for you and Bracewell. Perhaps there is as much to the false Lord's story as there is to Mr Hewitt's. I hope, however, that my statement will exonerate the unfortunate postman and allow him to rebuild his life, and I have an inkling that he might want to do that with Mrs Kemp.

Amelia Forman

After a brief discussion with Lestrade, Holmes turned to Amelia and said, "You are free to go. The inspector wishes to talk to Hewitt, but your statement should secure his release."

"Thank you both," said Miss Forman. "I expect that my employment with the Bracewells will shortly come to an end, so I shall return home."

"Our business here is concluded," said Holmes. "But our work is not yet complete. There is another mystery that requires our attention and – for that – we must return to Baker Street to meet Gregson."

Now turn to page 204.

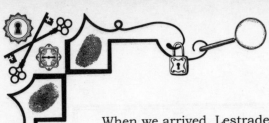

When we arrived, Lestrade was nowhere to be found. We introduced ourselves to the pub owner and asked if the inspector had left a message for us. The man lit a candle so as to take a good look at us. It was clear that he had been told to expect us, but for good or for ill?

At length, he broke his silence: "Yes, a man with the face of a ferret waited for you for a very long time. He described you," motioning to Holmes, "but made no mention that you would have company. He left you this message, saying that you would know what to do with it. I'll be right back – I need to check on a delivery." He handed Holmes a slip of paper, and then headed to the back of the building.

Holmes read the note aloud: "If this is who I think it is, order a drink in the colour of spring containing peaseblossom, cobweb, moth and mustardseed. All shall be revealed. – L'."

"That does not sound appetising, Holmes," I said, wincing at the ingredients. "What does Lestrade mean to accomplish by having us drink such a concoction?"

"It's another riddle," said Holmes, eyebrows raised thoughtfully.

"I would not have thought Lestrade so well read," mused Holmes. "Let us break down this most recent message. To order a drink in the colour of spring is obviously a clue that the liquid will be green in colour. Peaseblossom, cobweb, moth and mustardseed are not ingredients. They are the faeries who attend Queen Titania in the play *A Midsummer Night's Dream*. Green faeries, or, more specifically, The Green Fairy, is a byname for absinthe. Let us find the appropriate bottle of absinthe,

What drink are they supposed to order?

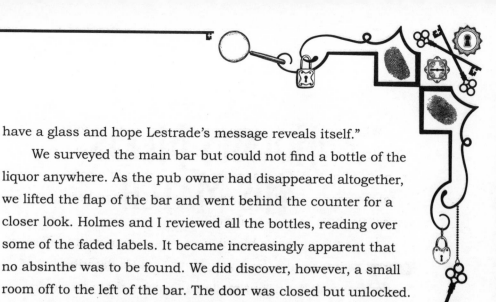

have a glass and hope Lestrade's message reveals itself."

We surveyed the main bar but could not find a bottle of the liquor anywhere. As the pub owner had disappeared altogether, we lifted the flap of the bar and went behind the counter for a closer look. Holmes and I reviewed all the bottles, reading over some of the faded labels. It became increasingly apparent that no absinthe was to be found. We did discover, however, a small room off to the left of the bar. The door was closed but unlocked. We walked into a room, the walls of which were covered with shelves and shelves of bottles.

As the door closed behind us, I heard a small click. It seemed immaterial, deep as we were in our quest to locate the correct bottle of spirits. I removed a dusty, unlabelled bottle of a milky-white liquid from a small shelf just inside the door. It was three-quarters full and its top was completely sealed with wax. I eyed it with some curiosity.

"Aha!" shouted Holmes, nearly making me drop the bottle. I hastily returned it to the shelf, as he picked up a bottle of the bright-green liquid from the shelf before him. A second click sounded, much louder than the first, and Holmes reached into the space behind it to retrieve a small package addressed to him in Lestrade's handwriting. Holmes replaced the bottle of absinthe on the shelf, and we made our way to the door, only to find it securely locked.

We were trapped!

Now turn to page 107.

HOLMES MEETS HIS MATCH

"We are heading to London's West End, right near Piccadilly Circus," Holmes confirmed.

"The sooner we work out whom to trust, Watson, the sooner we shall find the children. The job agency, Cromwell's, is the crucial link between the Bracewells and Miss Forman. Surely you must be wondering why Lord Bracewell hired a governess, even one as capable as Miss Forman, for such an exorbitant sum. Her salary is much higher than that of a standard governess, which is equivalent to the number of our Majesty's children multiplied by the number of elite guardsmen at the beginning of Dumas' novel. What qualifications does she have and who recommended her to Bracewell and Mrs Clemens?"

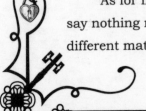

What is the typical annual salary for a governess at this time?

"I've no idea what novel you're referring to, Holmes," I said. "What shall we tell our host?"

"You've never read *The Three Musketeers*, Watson?" Holmes shook his head incredulously at the thought.

"Queen Victoria had nine children, and when you multiple them by the *three* musketeers, it comes to twenty-seven pounds.

"As for informing our host of our whereabouts, we shall say nothing more than is strictly necessary. Let us say that a different matter – the museum affair, for example – takes us

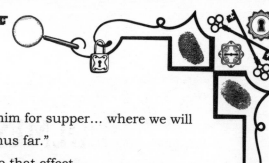

to London, and we hope to join him for supper... where we will apprise him of our discoveries thus far."

We left a note for our host to that effect.

The streets were buzzing with activity as vendors plied their wares; and the sounds contrasted strikingly with the quietness of Finchley. We were surprised to meet PC Gregson at the storefront of Cromwell's. Gregson towers even over Holmes, and he was preparing to deliver an address to a small crowd of excited journalists, all vying for his attention with their questions. It was as much as his fellow police officers could do to restrain them from entering the shop.

Gregson stopped when he saw us and ushered us inside.

"There's bad business, Mr Holmes!" he said, shaking our hands. "I am so glad to see you, and you too, Dr Watson."

"What is the matter?" asked my friend, when we reached an inner room.

"Did you not get my note? I wrote to Baker Street not twenty minutes ago."

"Gregson, even you should know that would have been completely impossible," said Holmes.

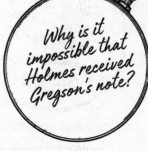

Why is it impossible that Holmes received Gregson's note?

"Whatever do you mean, Holmes? I sent a messenger not twenty minutes ago and here you stand before me," argued Gregson.

Holmes sighed. "If you sent the message only twenty minutes ago – and it would take even the quickest messenger by cab at least twelve minutes to get to Baker Street – we would have needed to read your message, gather ourselves up and then make our way here. It would have taken us at least thirty minutes to reach you.

"However, by fortunate coincidence, we have convened in the same place at the same time. We have been... away." Holmes waved his hand.

"You are such a stickler for details," grumbled Gregson. "But I am glad that you are here, regardless of the circumstance. There was a burglary. That man there is Mr Cromwell, the proprietor and the lady is Miss Stoper, who works with him." He nodded at the other two occupants of the little office. "Give me a few moments to get the scene outside under some sort of control and I will rejoin you presently."

We sat down in the small sitting room inside the main door and could see the two persons in the adjoining room. Mr Cromwell was an elderly man, who, even amongst such chaos, had his nose deep in the most recent release from Walter Besant. Thick spectacles perched on the end of his nose and clawed hands clutched his novel. We had been waiting for about ten minutes when I observed Mr Cromwell grumble at having lost his page after dropping the book on the floor multiple times.

Miss Stoper, in contrast, appeared a sensible character. Her hair was in a tight bun and her large spectacles ensured she didn't miss a thing as she tidied her desk – which appeared in almost perfect symmetry. She sat with perfect posture, clothes perfectly pressed, with a generally tidy appearance – something one would perhaps expect of a lady whose job it is to assess the abilities of potential governesses.

"Mr Cromwell should invest in a new desk and pair of glasses," remarked Holmes. "I'm surprised Miss Stoper puts up with him all day long."

"What do you mean?" I asked him. "For what reason would Mr Cromwell need a new desk?"

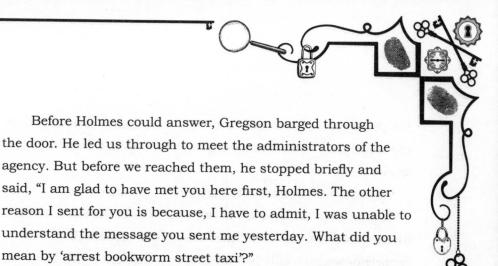

Before Holmes could answer, Gregson barged through the door. He led us through to meet the administrators of the agency. But before we reached them, he stopped briefly and said, "I am glad to have met you here first, Holmes. The other reason I sent for you is because, I have to admit, I was unable to understand the message you sent me yesterday. What did you mean by 'arrest bookworm street taxi'?"

"I thought that even you would be able to solve a simple anagram, Gregson. I asked you to meet us at Baker Street at six tomorrow, which would now be this evening. I will need to speak with you later. I'll leave you with additional instructions, should we be delayed."

"I'll see you tonight then. Let's now take care of this business," said Gregson, and we turned towards Miss Stoper and Mr Cromwell.

"What was stolen?" Gregson asked of them both. Mr Cromwell dropped his book again.

"You'd best direct your questions to me," said Miss Stoper. "Mr Cromwell is here to do the books, but he spends most of his days reading Mr Besant's latest works. I essentially run the business now. I have raised the profile of this agency over the last few years – the people we recommend are now in high demand among all classes throughout London. I am the *youngest* employment administrator in the city, a fact which I take great pride in. I started working here as a secretary, at the age of eighteen, after years of my own rigorous education. I was home-schooled by my father, who was a teacher at Eton."

"Quite an accomplishment, my dear lady," said Holmes. "But can you tell us what happened? What was stolen?"

"Something of immense value!" Miss Stoper exclaimed.

She peered at us through her glasses. I felt her intense scrutiny and pitied the young women who interviewed with her. "Who are you two?"

Holmes and I introduced ourselves.

"That's not what I mean," she insisted, "I am asking what your professions are. I can tell that you are not from Scotland Yard. You don't have the bearing."

"I am a medical doctor," I explained, "And my friend..." I was at a loss for words.

"I am a consulting detective. I help the police with their puzzles. Now, again, Miss Stoper, please do tell us what has been stolen."

"My files!" she said, thrusting her open-palmed hands towards us, as if the value of these items was self-evident. When her answer had little impact on us, she explained further. "They contain private information about our clients, who trust in our discretion. In the wrong hands, it is likely that the company will be ruined. All my years of hard work will be for nothing!"

Myself, I could not see the value in the addresses of, and correspondence with, a few dozen people – no matter their pedigree. I could see that Gregson shared my feelings on the matter. Holmes, however, became quite agitated.

"How many files were taken?" he asked.

"All of them. Imagine how valuable they could be to our competitors!"

"No doubt!" my friend observed. "Has such a theft happened here before?"

"Never, not in the seventeen years that I have worked here – since the beginning of the summer I left my family home. There is no time to lose, Mr Holmes. I have my eye on the Colleys, an agency that opened recently down the street. You should investigate them immediately. They will have heard rumours that Mr Cromwell is planning to retire and close his business – whereas I am hoping he will allow me to continue on his behalf. It seems that they can't wait for the clients to sign up with them of their own accord and I refuse to work for anyone else."

Gregson dutifully noted this down.

"When did the burglary happen?" he asked.

"It could have happened any time between closing hour, at 6 p.m., and this morning. I arrived at the office by 7 a.m. as always."

"The burglar had around 12 hours?"

"Indeed."

"Are the premises locked overnight?"

"Locked and bolted. I keep all my files in the metal safe. I locked it myself using a combination that I change every year – it is something that only I would know. A copy of the combination is in our safe deposit box at the bank, which can only be accessed by myself and Mr Cromwell. The safe was perfectly secure and Miss French, my assistant, locked the inner and the outer offices as we left together last night. I watched her do it and nothing was improper. We arrived this morning to find the window broken."

We looked around the small office. It did not take us long, for it was clear how the culprit broke in: glass from the broken window had been left behind, both inside and outside the building. Holmes inspected the lock, the door and the window in turn. He made a note in his journal and turned back to us.

Regarding the lock, he clarified with Miss Stoper: "How often do you change the combination on this safe?"

"Yearly. Although I changed it last month as I don't trust those scoundrels down the street."

"Thank you," Holmes said, "but your combination isn't as safe as you hope. Anyone in possession of a few details about you could tell that you are proud of your accomplishments, you have a preference for logic, balance and symmetry, and the combination is likely be personal, yet something you can change on a regular basis. That makes it entirely predictable."

Holmes bent down to the safe. I watched as he struggled to spin the heavy dial several times. It proceeded to open on his first attempt.

How did Holmes deduce the combination?

"How did you do that?" Miss Stoper cried. She threw the papers she had been holding onto the floor in a fit of rage.

I couldn't help but notice the ornate text on the top of the letterhead, spelling out "Cromwell's".

Cromwell's

EMPLOYMENT AGENCY

150 Beak Street, London W1F 9RN

Holmes explained himself: "You provided a detailed background about yourself as we were introduced. You

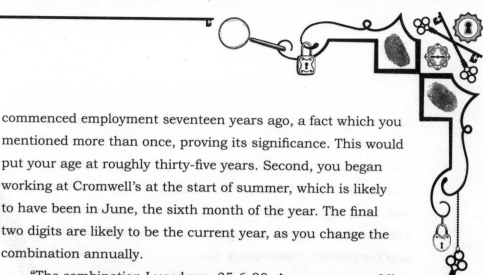

commenced employment seventeen years ago, a fact which you mentioned more than once, proving its significance. This would put your age at roughly thirty-five years. Second, you began working at Cromwell's at the start of summer, which is likely to have been in June, the sixth month of the year. The final two digits are likely to be the current year, as you change the combination annually.

"The combination I used was 35-6-90. As you can see, Miss Stoper, I'm sure many who have spoken to you would be able to extract these details from you, unbeknownst to you of course. You told us these things without prompting.

"Getting the order correct on my first try, however," he turned to me and winked, "was pure luck." At the sound of that, I began to chuckle, but covered it with a cough.

Holmes turned back to Miss Stoper.

"Watson and I are here on a different matter, though. Do you remember a client by the name of Bracewell?"

Incredulously, Miss Stoper smiled: "I remember every client who inquires with us and every governess who visits this office. I am in no need of physical files to recall this, Mr Holmes. I won't forget this particular business soon. There was something off about it."

"Why?"

"You see, Mr Holmes, there was very little correspondence between his representative, a Mrs Clemens, and our agency. It is not uncommon for rich men and their families to approach us through a senior servant; they often have pressing business and are not always in a position where they can visit us directly.

"Mrs Clemens visited us one afternoon and, sitting on the chair where Mr Cromwell is presently sat, she spelled out

her employer's terms. The sum she offered was exceptionally high and I can honestly say that it was the best offer I have known in all my years working here. I myself was tempted to take the position. It's rare, but not completely unheard of, for an employer to offer a high salary to attract the best talent within the first year and to then work out a more equitable arrangement after the term of the initial contract is reached. But this was a once-in-a-lifetime offer.

"But there is more to it: normally, a prospective employer – or his or her representative – would want to interview the governess him- or herself, and at the very least they would check the references. However, Mrs Clemens made it clear that she trusted my judgement and was in great haste to make the hire without meeting the governess."

"Did you have any suspicions?"

Miss Stoper took a deep breath. "There was little I could do. I had asked Miss French to visit the Bracewell house, to provide a letter of introduction and to meet with his Lordship and the children. I was too occupied in the office to join her. She met with Lord Bracewell and delivered my letter, talked with the children, and the situation seemed as Mrs Clemens described it. It behoved us to find a suitable governess. She returned with Lord Bracewell's assent to find a governess and was instructed to work with Mrs Clemens to find the right candidate."

"What can you tell us about Miss Forman?"

"She was a very good nursery governess despite her limited practical experience. The reference from her previous family was excellent and we have had no complaints about her."

"Have you known her long?"

"For only about two years. The poor girl – ever since her

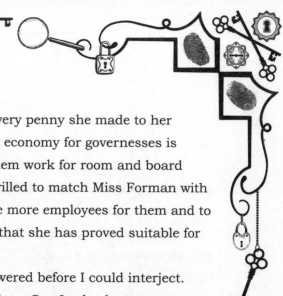

stepfather died, she has sent every penny she made to her family, but it wasn't much. The economy for governesses is terrible, Mr Holmes. Many of them work for room and board without even a salary. I was thrilled to match Miss Forman with the Bracewells. I hope to secure more employees for them and to become their top agent. I trust that she has proved suitable for the children?"

"Perfectly so," Holmes answered before I could interject.

"Good! I expected nothing less. Can I ask why you are asking about this case?"

"Enough with this nonsense!" burst out Gregson, before Holmes could reply. We looked at the angry policeman. "You are under arrest, Stoper and Cromwell!" The shout made Mr Cromwell drop his book again in shock.

"But why?" Holmes wondered.

"You must see why," Gregson said.

Holmes and I looked at each other in wonder.

"Miss Stoper stole the files herself!"

We were too stunned to reply, but Gregson needed no encouragement.

"And Cromwell abetted her."

"But why would they steal their own files?"

"That's for them to tell us – at the police station!"

"But you have made no charges," I protested.

Holmes continued: "And Cromwell couldn't steal his own files even if he wanted to because he wouldn't be able to open the safe."

Why is Mr Cromwell unable to open the safe?

Gregson stopped where he stood, while Cromwell fainted in his chair.

"Holmes," I said gently, "did you forget that Miss Stoper said her combination is in the bank safe that only she and Mr Cromwell can access it?"

"Watson," sighed Holmes. "Cromwell would not be able to turn the heavy dial to input the combination. I even had difficulty entering the combination myself."

"This makes no sense. Why wouldn't Cromwell be able to turn the dial?" asked Gregson.

"Look at his hands. They are pulled into claws and he keeps dropping his book. His hands are afflicted with severe arthritis, so turning such a heavy dial with the precision needed to input a combination would be close to impossible. You've made a mistake, Gregson."

"I tried to tell you that it was the Colleys," Miss Stoper cried. "I'm innocent!"

"Of the theft, perhaps," interjected Holmes. "But you are not fully innocent. You have also provided us with a motive as to the disposition of the files."

What is Miss Stoper's motivation for setting up the theft?

"What motive?" asked Miss Stoper. "I've been a loyal employee for seventeen years."

"And that loyalty is coming to an end now that Cromwell is closing his business. You pride yourself on what you've done for the business and can't abide the fact that he will not turn the agency over to you. So, you made a deal with Bracewell: he provides you with the money to start up your own agency and, in return, you provide him with servants when he needs replacements.

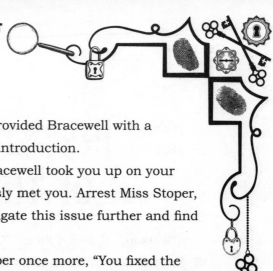

Miss French unknowingly provided Bracewell with a proposition instead of a letter of introduction.

"But the question is why Bracewell took you up on your offer when he had never previously met you. Arrest Miss Stoper, Gregson. We shall need to investigate this issue further and find the missing files."

Holmes addressed Miss Stoper once more, "You fixed the crime scene upon your arrival this morning by ensuring there was glass on both sides of the window, so that we would not be able to tell if the glass was broken by someone trying to get in, or by someone concealed inside trying to get out. In either case, the files are gone and must be recovered. They might provide some insight into the matters before us."

Miss Stoper protested her innocence. As Gregson held her arms, she turned towards the unconscious Mr Cromwell as she was led to the door. "This is all your fault," she said. "I gave you everything and you didn't care to return the favour, you dotty old man."

"Gregson, before you take her away," Holmes said, "I have one final question. Miss Stoper, if you choose to cooperate, anything you can tell us will be taken into consideration when charges are filed against you. Can you tell us anything about Lord Bracewell himself?"

"Lord Bracewell is in Australia—" was all Miss Stoper managed to say before Gregson herded her away.

Now turn to page 147.

THE STATEMENT OF THE CASE

You could cut the silence in the room with a knife. The large clock chimed two o'clock.

"Here is a map of the crime scene," Lestrade said. "I have marked the site of the carriage with an 'X'. This, here, is Westwood Manor. Bracewell's estate is a short walk northwest from the small village of Totteridge. As you can see, the carriage was only about two miles away from its destination when it came to a stop."

Holmes and I studied it closely and I made a copy.

"Who discovered the unhappy scene?" he asked.

"A postman on his round. Name of George Hewitt. He was a hundred feet or so away from the crime scene. Between the rain and his short-sightedness, though, he could scarce make out the carriage. According to his report, the rain and the mist made visibility impossible, with or without his glasses."

"Did he hear the gunshot?"

Lestrade smiled as he withdrew his notebook from his coat pocket and flipped through its pages. "You see, Mr Holmes, I had asked all of the questions that you would if you had been there. Hewitt heard the shot indeed. It frightened him and his horses."

"Was the Bracewells' carriage stationary?"

"Yes. Hewitt nearly crashed into it. The horses themselves stopped suddenly, which almost threw him from the carriage. He had almost calmed them when the gunshot went off, spooking them all over again. It took him a while to placate them and

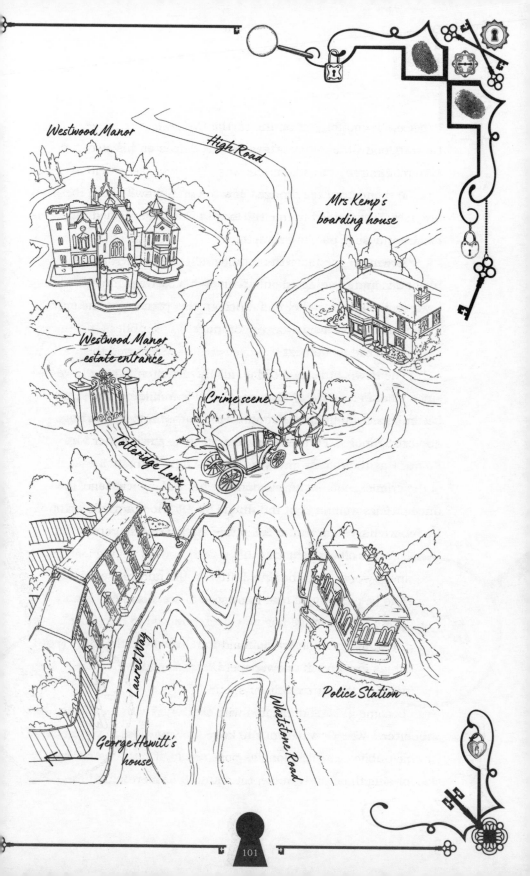

Westwood Manor

High Road

Mrs Kemp's
boarding house

Westwood Manor
estate entrance

Crime scene

Totteridge Lane

Laurel Way

George Hewitt's
house

Whetstone Road

Police Station

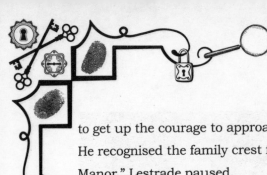

to get up the courage to approach the Bracewells' carriage. He recognised the family crest from his deliveries to Westwood Manor." Lestrade paused.

"You can even see the coat of arms on the wall above the fireplace." He nodded to the wall across from him. "The family has been a huge part of this area.

"Hewitt stepped into the mud, which reached the top of his boots, and running one hand along his carriage, he moved towards the one ahead of him. Without this precaution, he may never have found his way to the carriage."

"What did he do next?"

"There was little he could do for the driver, whom we have since identified as Harry Mullins. Out of fear of the crime scene becoming contaminated, he moved the corpse into the carriage and brought Miss Forman, the governess, to the home of Mrs Kemp, a gentlewoman who lives about a mile and a half east of the crime scene. As he was moving her into his carriage, the unconscious woman kept mumbling about 'the tips of the arrows'. He reported the incident at the police station in Whetstone and the officer sent for me.

"By the time I arrived, the rain had washed away all that there was to see. The unfortunate carriage has now been removed to the police station for examination. I removed the diary that I myself discovered," Lestrade paused for effect, "at the crime scene."

Where did Lestrade find Amelia's diary?

"Well done!" Holmes exclaimed with a smile, as he shook the inspector's hand. "You have truly surpassed yourself: you have put your thirst for the truth ahead of your customary zeal for action. Let me guess? You found the diary behind the

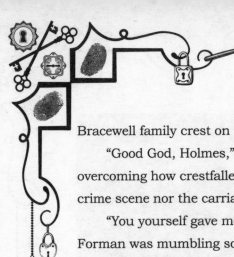

Bracewell family crest on the carriage."

"Good God, Holmes," gasped the inspector, his awe overcoming how crestfallen he was. "You have seen neither the crime scene nor the carriage. How did you know?"

"You yourself gave me the location. You mentioned that Miss Forman was mumbling something about 'the tips of the arrows'. The Bracewell family crest includes two silver chevrons, which fit that description. If I had only been there to investigate the rest of the scene! I could have read much into the tracks, including how long the carriage had stopped for and why. Doubtless, the police trampled over all of the evidence when they removed the carriage. Was Mr Hewitt informed of the missing children?"

"No. In fact, we did not know that the children and their dog were missing until we read Miss Forman's diary: she has been feverish since the ordeal and we are yet to question her."

"Has there been any word from the abductors?"

"None. Holmes, I must confess, I am at my wits' end. There are puzzles aplenty, but the threads are far too tangled. For now, we have managed to keep this sad affair a secret from the newspapers, and it is better this way: reporters poking into this business would only confuse matters more and cause vital clues to be concealed. Who knows what the morrow will bring?"

"I quite agree, Lestrade," said Holmes. "Much as I rely on the newspapers, particularly the agony columns, our jobs will become more complicated with prying reporters. We will endeavour to keep this out of the public eye for as long as possible. It is surprising that you have kept it a secret for more

How long has Lestrade kept the crime out of the papers?

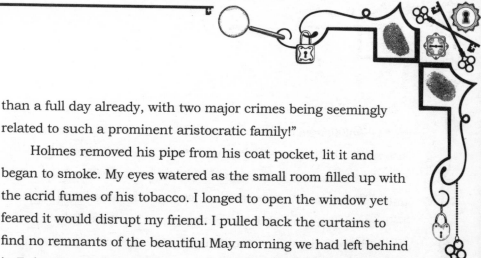

than a full day already, with two major crimes being seemingly related to such a prominent aristocratic family!"

Holmes removed his pipe from his coat pocket, lit it and began to smoke. My eyes watered as the small room filled up with the acrid fumes of his tobacco. I longed to open the window yet feared it would disrupt my friend. I pulled back the curtains to find no remnants of the beautiful May morning we had left behind in Baker Street. Once more, it was pouring, and the rains pattered on the roof and pelted heavily against the windowpane. When the public house landlord, Mr Welsh, came in with another lamp, Holmes ordered sandwiches and coffee, reminding me of how hungry I was. We had eaten nothing since our hasty breakfast, and supper seemed distant as we brooded over the mystery.

When Welsh returned with our food, Holmes thanked him and inquired: "My friend and I are not from these parts, yet we have heard much about the charms of Westwood Manor. We hope to visit the estate this afternoon. Do you know it?"

"Like the back of my hand. My mother, God rest her soul, was housekeeper and I was friends with the present Lord Bracewell's father, Cecil. But alas, you have come at a bad time!"

The landlord's response startled Lestrade but a look from Holmes prevented the inspector from saying what was on his mind.

"And why is that?" Holmes asked.

How old were the children when their mother died?

"I only meant that Lord Bracewell hasn't been himself these past years. You would have had a warmer welcome five years ago when Lady Bracewell was alive. You see, my good sirs, the Lord and Lady were very much in love, but her death was the final straw that broke the young man."

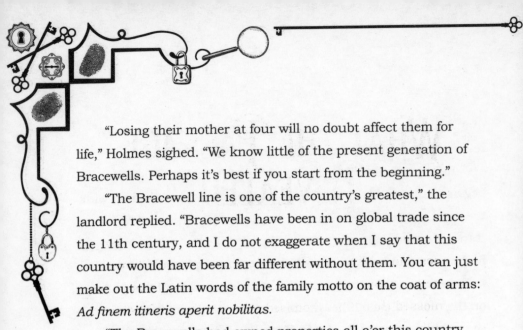

"Losing their mother at four will no doubt affect them for life," Holmes sighed. "We know little of the present generation of Bracewells. Perhaps it's best if you start from the beginning."

"The Bracewell line is one of the country's greatest," the landlord replied. "Bracewells have been in on global trade since the 11th century, and I do not exaggerate when I say that this country would have been far different without them. You can just make out the Latin words of the family motto on the coat of arms: *Ad finem itineris aperit nobilitas*.

"The Bracewells had owned properties all o'er this country and many beyond. But Lord Bracewell's grandfather, Edward, was a wicked'un. He squandered, gambled and speculated away much of the family fortune, and made the lives of his wife and son a misery."

What is the Bracewell family motto?

"Ironic that the old Lord Bracewell forgot to live by his own family motto, no?" said Holmes, with a whistle.

Choose from one of the three options:

Nobility is conferred on those who seize it.

If you think this is the motto, turn to page 30.

If you think this is the motto, turn to page 30.

Nobility begins at the journey's end.

If you think this is the motto, turn to page 196.

Eternal nobility belongs to those upon whom it is conferred.

If you think this is the motto, turn to page 203.

WHAT THE PACKAGE REVEALED

Holmes and I did what you, my dear reader, would have done: we shouted for help. Were I less honest, I would not have confessed this, but I promised to report Holmes's activities as faithfully as possible – even if we risk losing your admiration. The thick walls muffled our cries and our hammering on the door went unnoticed. Dejected, after a while, we began to survey the room. There was the single door we had entered through, with a small keyhole and a small round window 10 feet from the ground – far too small for anyone to crawl through. The room was illuminated by a lantern and I prayed fervently that it carried sufficient oil to keep the room lit for as long as would be necessary.

Holmes studied the keyhole. "There is no lock," he observed. He peered through the crack between the door and frame and found that the door was secured by small bolts.

"A key would not help us here."

I looked over at the small rectangular table near the door, which was inset with seven slats of wood and a series of curious markings.

"What do you make of these?" I asked.

"Clearly, they are the first half of the lunar cycle," Holmes said. The connection was not immediately apparent to me, but I nodded in agreement as I stroked my chin.

"What does it mean?"

"That is for us to discover," Holmes replied.

"Do you see any reference to the Moon or the lunar cycle in this room?"

We looked around and inspected the bottles once more, but this time for references, however tangential, to the Moon. Nothing about the names or liquors suggested anything lunar.

How did Holmes unlock the door?

Holmes paused by the door, stared at the unlabelled bottle I had replaced moments before and exclaimed, "Aha! I shall soon have us out."

Holmes removed the bottle of white liquid and set it in the blank space in the waxing gibbous Moon phase (three-quarters white). We heard a loud click. Holmes turned the doorknob and the door opened easily. He returned the bottle to its original position.

Holmes and I left the room and returned to the pub.

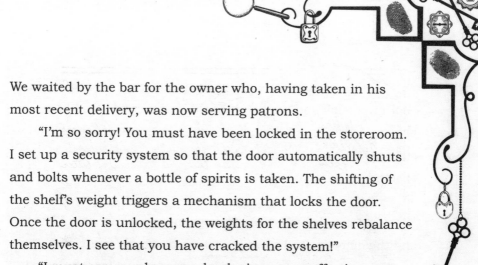

We waited by the bar for the owner who, having taken in his most recent delivery, was now serving patrons.

"I'm so sorry! You must have been locked in the storeroom. I set up a security system so that the door automatically shuts and bolts whenever a bottle of spirits is taken. The shifting of the shelf's weight triggers a mechanism that locks the door. Once the door is unlocked, the weights for the shelves rebalance themselves. I see that you have cracked the system!"

"I must commend you on developing a very effective anti-theft mechanism. It is unique! You could make a small fortune from it," Holmes said enthusiastically. "Let me guess: the wax seal is to prevent the liquid from evaporating and the bottle's weight from changing."

"Exactly!"

"We have reset the puzzle and returned the 'key' to its shelf," Holmes said.

I directed us to the problem at hand by motioning to Lestrade's package: "We have been somewhat delayed from our task. Can you direct us to one of your private rooms?"

The proprietor, who identified himself as Mr Welsh, led us to a room where Holmes and I sat at opposite ends of a small table with the parcel between us. He tore the shopkeepers' paper to remove a brown leather book, secured with a stout red ribbon. Holmes leafed through the pages, only a few of which had been written on. He scrutinised the neat and precise writing. I saw his nose crinkle as he held the diary close to his face and inhaled.

Why was Holmes reviewing the diary so closely and what did he discover?

"This tells us about the owner," Holmes said.

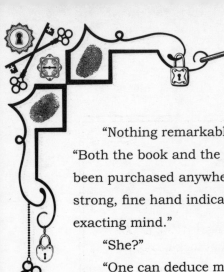

"Nothing remarkable about the stationery," he continued. "Both the book and the pen that the writer used could have been purchased anywhere. Her pen is in excellent repair. The strong, fine hand indicates that she possesses a firm and exacting mind."

"She?"

"One can deduce much from penmanship, my dear Watson, and the detective-to-be would make a profitable study of it. The owner has not been in possession of the journal for long: this is apparent both from the sparsity of the entries and from the whiff of fragrance that you can just catch if you hold the paper to your nose. Let us see what Lestrade and the author wish to tell us."

Holmes opened the book and read aloud:

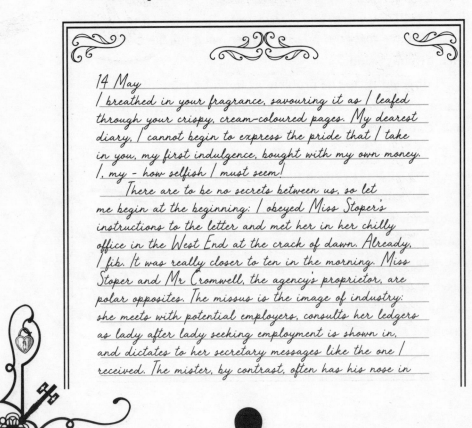

14 May

I breathed in your fragrance, savouring it as I leafed through your crispy, cream-coloured pages. My dearest diary, I cannot begin to express the pride that I take in you, my first indulgence, bought with my own money. I, my – how selfish I must seem!

There are to be no secrets between us, so let me begin at the beginning: I obeyed Miss Stoper's instructions to the letter and met her in her chilly office in the West End at the crack of dawn. Already, I fib. It was really closer to ten in the morning. Miss Stoper and Mr Cromwell, the agency's proprietor, are polar opposites. The missus is the image of industry: she meets with potential employers, consults her ledgers as lady after lady seeking employment is shown in, and dictates to her secretary messages like the one I received. The mister, by contrast, often has his nose in a book. This morning was no different. He was possibly dabbing his eyes as he pored over the latest by George Gissing.

My meeting with Miss Stoper was brief and to the point. Her eyes were darting over my application even as she posed questions.

Stoper: Are you still looking for a situation as a governess?

Me: Yes, ma'am.

S: Êtes-vous suffisamment compétente pour enseigner aux petits enfants?

M: Bien sûr Madame! Je parle très bien français. La dernière famille pour qui j'ai travaillé passait souvent l'été à Paris. Les enfants recevaient donc des enseignements quotidiens. Mon père est français.

S: Are you proficient with the three Rs?

M: Yes, reading, writing and arithmetic.

S: How about drawing?

M: Yes, ma'am.

S: Good, and I see that your former employers held you in high regard. I have an excellent situation: the Bracewells in Finchley need a nursery-governess for their twins Charlie and Matilda, aged nine. [Here, she paused.]

One final test: only one month has the same number of letters as its placement in the year; multiply that number by the number of English kings named Henry and then add a baker's dozen - that will be your annual salary.

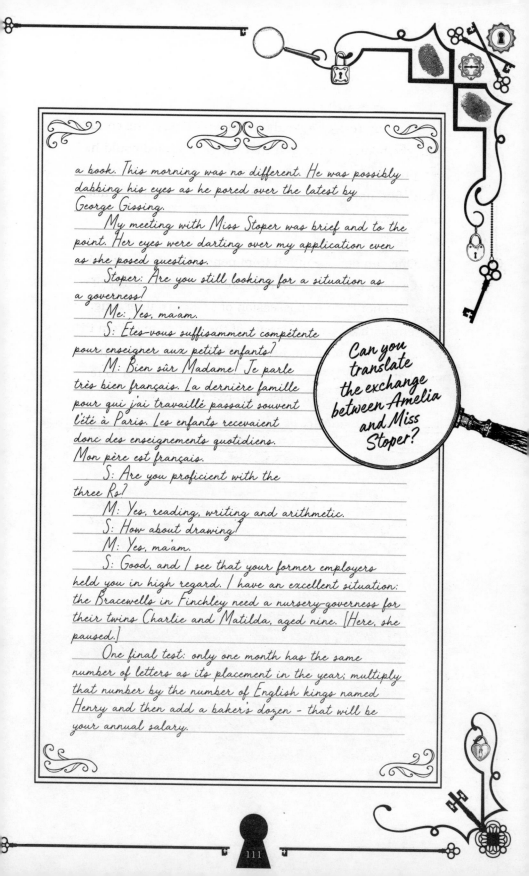

Can you translate the exchange between Amelia and Miss Stoper?

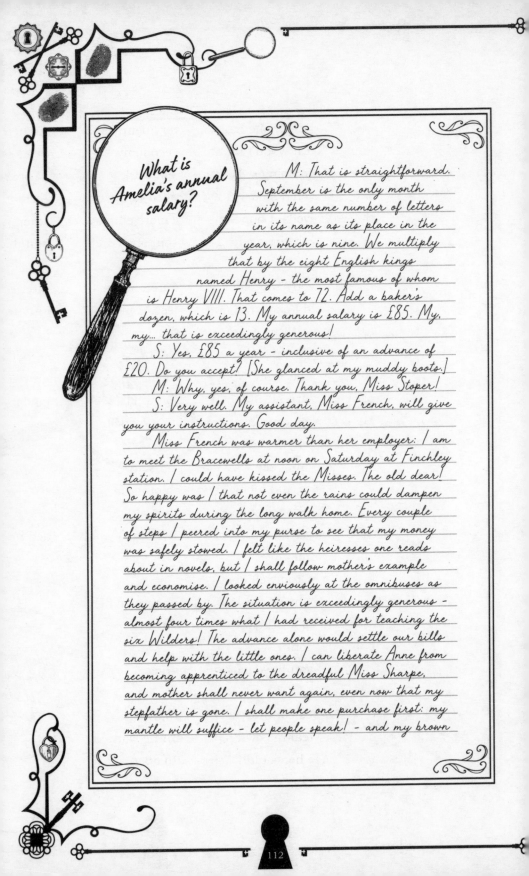

What is Amelia's annual salary?

M: That is straightforward. September is the only month with the same number of letters in its name as its place in the year, which is nine. We multiply that by the eight English kings named Henry - the most famous of whom is Henry VIII. That comes to 72. Add a baker's dozen, which is 13. My annual salary is £85. My, my... that is exceedingly generous!

S: Yes, £85 a year - inclusive of an advance of £20. Do you accept? [She glanced at my muddy boots.]

M: Why, yes, of course. Thank you, Miss Stoper!

S: Very well. My assistant, Miss French, will give you your instructions. Good day.

Miss French was warmer than her employer: I am to meet the Bracewells at noon on Saturday at Finchley station. I could have kissed the Misses. The old dear! So happy was I that not even the rains could dampen my spirits during the long walk home. Every couple of steps I peered into my purse to see that my money was safely stowed. I felt like the heiresses one reads about in novels, but I shall follow mother's example and economise. I looked enviously at the omnibuses as they passed by. The situation is exceedingly generous - almost four times what I had received for teaching the six Wilders! The advance alone would settle our bills and help with the little ones. I can liberate Anne from becoming apprenticed to the dreadful Miss Sharpe, and mother shall never want again, even now that my stepfather is gone. I shall make one purchase first: my mantle will suffice - let people speak! - and my brown

straw hat and I have weathered many a storm together. But I do so want a diary, a bosom companion with whom I can share my every adventure and secret. To be so far from home and to be leaving so soon! I shall write Anne and mother every day, twice Sundays, so they need not miss me as much as I will them.

Holmes paused and his eyes wandered; but I entreated him to continue.

16 May

My dearest diary, I promise to be a better correspondent: I will not be one of those writers who can only keep up their diaries for one or two days. There was, and there is, so much to do before the big day (tomorrow)! I prepared lessons and bought copybooks for the youngest darlings so that they can study under Anne, who, in my absence, is now promoted to the role of big sister. I feel as if I haven't slept a wink since my appointment. I wonder what the Bracewell children - Charlie and Matilda - are like and if they are as excited to meet me as I am them. I have even created an activity for them.

Anne gave me her gloves, and mother her handkerchief, despite my firm assurances that I want for nothing. My clothes were mended and pressed and my bag packed. I shall sleep well tonight and be ready for anything tomorrow.

17 May

This long entry will make up for the brevity of its predecessor. After kissing mother and the young ones twice each, I left to catch my train. I was halfway to the station when I remembered you, my treasured (and only) companion, securely hidden to protect you from prying eyes. I have recently offered to sweep the floor of my room myself. When mother asked why, I told her that the intersecting of the boards in the middle of the room reminded me of a reference to Treasure Island, which is one of my favourite stories.

I ran all the way home. I retrieved you from my hiding place under the floorboard at the centre of the X in our bedroom (X marks the spot, yet is hidden in plain sight), kissed everyone a third time and made for the station. I arrived more soaked than ever, but on time! Once seated, I withdrew from my bag my well-thumbed copy of A Tale of Two Cities, which I read until we reached the stop.

Finchley! I got off and looked around. I didn't have to wander far before I found Charlie and Matilda, the latter holding a small spaniel - named, I was to learn, Spot. I rushed to greet them, and in her excitement, Matilda released Spot, who raced around the station. We gave chase, found Spot and lost Matilda. When Spot and I found her, Charlie had vanished.

By the time every member of our party was accounted for and properly introduced, we were all

Where is Amelia's treasured diary hidden? How do you know?

breathless from the laughing and running. Not a bad way to meet one's charges, I would say! By sheer coincidence, their hiding places matched a significant day in my life! How funny fate can be, for I am sure we will become great friends.

    The driver held an umbrella over us as he assisted us into the carriage, even stopping to offer Spot a treat and a pat on the head to encourage him to jump inside. We got in the carriage and away we went to Westwood Manor. I say went, but really, we were inching forward slowly. The coachman and the animals, poor beasts, stoically battled the mighty winds, the rain pelting us all the way. The children and I sat comfortably in our passenger seat and played with Spot. I asked about their home and their family, but they became shy and reticent now that they were seated across from me.

At this moment there came a knock on our door and Lestrade, as ferret-like as ever, appeared. The inspector greeted us warmly and took a seat between us.

"Lestrade. Now that you have arrived," said Holmes, as he promptly closed the book, "You can state the case."

"I see that you have found the puzzle I left for you. Were you able to retrieve it without too much difficulty?"

"It was straightforward."

"I will confess," he said with a grin, "I had hoped to find you still puzzled. I can only assume it didn't challenge you enough. Have you finished reading Miss Forman's diary?"

"The company is on its way to Westwood Manor," I said.

"There's not much left in the diary," said Lestrade. "Why don't you finish it, Mr Holmes?"

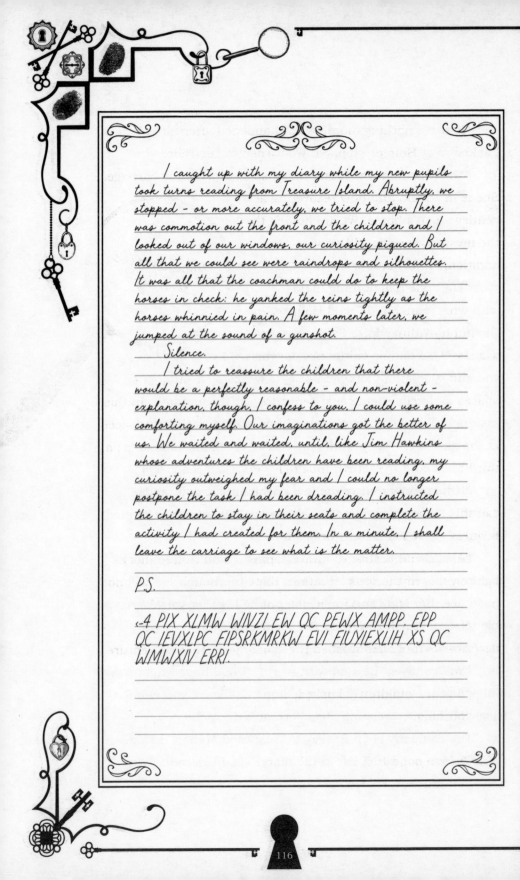

I caught up with my diary while my new pupils took turns reading from Treasure Island. Abruptly, we stopped - or more accurately, we tried to stop. There was commotion out the front and the children and I looked out of our windows, our curiosity piqued. But all that we could see were raindrops and silhouettes. It was all that the coachman could do to keep the horses in check: he yanked the reins tightly as the horses whinnied in pain. A few moments later, we jumped at the sound of a gunshot.

Silence.

I tried to reassure the children that there would be a perfectly reasonable - and non-violent - explanation, though, I confess to you, I could use some comforting myself. Our imaginations got the better of us. We waited and waited, until, like Jim Hawkins whose adventures the children have been reading, my curiosity outweighed my fear and I could no longer postpone the task I had been dreading. I instructed the children to stay in their seats and complete the activity I had created for them. In a minute, I shall leave the carriage to see what is the matter.

P.S.

,-4 PIX XLMW WIVZI EW QC PEWX AMPP. EPP QC IEVXLPC FIPSRKMRKW EVI FIUYIEXLIH XS QC WMWXIV ERRI.

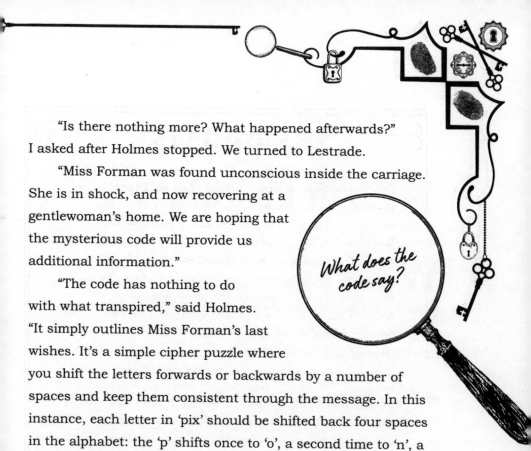

"Is there nothing more? What happened afterwards?" I asked after Holmes stopped. We turned to Lestrade.

"Miss Forman was found unconscious inside the carriage. She is in shock, and now recovering at a gentlewoman's home. We are hoping that the mysterious code will provide us additional information."

"The code has nothing to do with what transpired," said Holmes. "It simply outlines Miss Forman's last wishes. It's a simple cipher puzzle where you shift the letters forwards or backwards by a number of spaces and keep them consistent through the message. In this instance, each letter in 'pix' should be shifted back four spaces in the alphabet: the 'p' shifts once to 'o', a second time to 'n', a third to 'm' and the fourth time to 'l'. 'Pix' then reads 'Let'.

"If you apply that to the rest of the message, it reads: 'Let this serve as my last will. All my earthly belongings are bequeathed to my sister Anne'."

"Alas," said Lestrade. "I was hoping it would shed more light on this mysterious situation. Happily, though, we will not have to notify Miss Forman's sister of her final wishes."

"Let us finish reviewing the scene that Miss Forman described. The gunshot killed the coachman," Holmes ventured.

"Yes."

"And the children?" I asked.

"Missing."

Now turn to page 100.

The Mullins' in Mourning

We took the train east to Kent and arrived in Canterbury. The famous cathedral loomed before us as we left the railway station. We started walking and hoped to find someone who knew the Mullins family. We only knew from Mrs Clemens that they lived near the cathedral. After walking for about fifteen minutes, Holmes paused, pulled out his journal and began reviewing the dice puzzle, the compass and his name, as it had been written on the slip of paper in the dice cup. His eyes fell on the street sign at the next intersection.

"Watson," he smiled, "Mullins and the children weren't fortune-tellers predicting my assignment to this case. What I thought was my name on the slip of paper is actually the name of the road up ahead, and the compass has the 'N' circled."

I looked ahead and saw indeed that the street we were approaching was called N. Holmes Road.

"That is all well and good, Holmes," I said. "But are we to knock on every door on this street? There must be dozens of houses here."

"Now that I know the 'Holmes' in the dice game isn't referring to me, it will be straightforward to locate the home of the late Mr Mullins' parents."

Holmes showed me his journal. The sketch of the dice sat next to a compass with the direction N circled and an arrow pointing down.

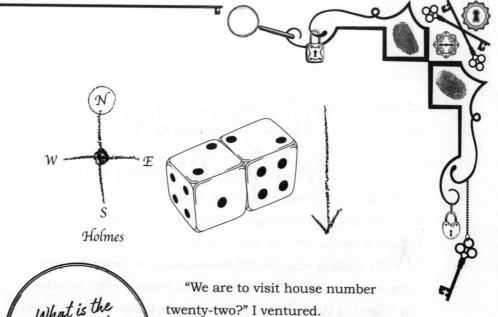

Holmes

What is the address of Harry Mullins's parents' house?

"We are to visit house number twenty-two?" I ventured.

"No, Watson," he said. "Mullins and the children would never make it that easy. You will have to look deeper than that, at the entire puzzle."

I looked again. After a few minutes, I told Holmes I was stumped.

"Ah, you give up too easily," chided Holmes, as he pulled out two dice that he had removed from the children's room and arranged them on his palm. "Look closely. The dice were placed in a very specific position. You can see the double twos are arranged so that one would be in the front on one of the dice and four would be in front on the other. Now that you have the dice in the position in the drawing, flip them towards you. Now, look at what is showing on top of the dice."

"A 6 and a 3, so 63," I sighed. "Why must they make everything so complicated?"

"The mind of a child can be more difficult than that of a criminal," agreed Holmes. "Let us be off to see Mr and Mrs Mullins at 63 North Holmes Road."

It was early afternoon by the time we arrived at Harry

Mullins's parents' cottage. The elderly Mrs Mullins opened the door. We introduced ourselves and explained why we had come.

"I am very sorry for your recent loss, Mrs Mullins," my friend said calmly. "My name is Sherlock Holmes and this is my friend and colleague Dr John Watson. I am a consulting detective and I am helping the police in their investigations regarding your son's death."

Mrs Mullins was dressed in mourning clothes, yet despite her grave expression, her face betrayed hints of genuine relief. She looked at Holmes with wonder as she led us into her house. Mr Mullins was at dinner wearing his old soldier's uniform, with the black armband of mourning.

"We welcome you, Mr Holmes and Dr Watson," said Mr Mullins. "I am Joshua Mullins and you have already met my wife, Hope. We will do our best to answer your questions, but while we mourn for Harry, I will be honest when I say that there is a great sense of relief that we will not have to continue supporting his bad decisions.

"He was a good lad, until he became an adult, and then sometime in his early twenties his demeanour just changed. Then he fell in with the wrong crowd... or should I say crowds. We've been anxious for him ever since two men visited—"

"Joshua!" Mrs Mullins hissed.

"Hope, there is no reason to conceal it from these gentlemen. An honest picture of Harry may hasten their investigations." He turned back to us. "Two men visited just a week ago and told us that we should remind Harry that M's patience has almost run out and he will be coming for his thousand pounds. I sent a messenger with what money I could scrape up to help him, figuring that even a partial payment to this 'M' might delay him from harm. We got word only last evening that Harry was found dead in Finchley. Perhaps he – and we – will now find peace."

Mrs Mullins's eyes glistened, but no tears fell, and she poured us tea from a well-worn kettle. The room in which we found ourselves was impeccably clean, though all of the furniture – from the table to chairs to bookcases – had seen better days. The wooden surfaces were in want of paint and polish and it was unclear whose chair was wobblier, Holmes's or mine. I dared not lean forward and I could tell that my friend, when seated, was similarly uncomfortable as he tried to adjust his preternatural height to the chair's confines. There were very few ornaments on display, but pictures had been given places

of prominence on the worn mantelpiece. Holmes stood and went over to look at a picture of Harry Mullins.

"We were given to understand that Harry had resigned from his position in the Bracewell household with the aim of repairing here to support you in your old age," said Holmes.

Mrs Mullins turned to her husband and replied, "Harry did resign, but it was not for our sake, as he told his employer, although that is what we believed at first too. He had debts, plenty of them. Harry had borrowed from the bad sort. Not all debts can be repaid with money."

"The bad sort?" Holmes repeated.

"He owed plenty of money, but he also owed favours to people who would not leave him in peace," Mr Mullins explained. "Let me try to give you a better picture of his character. Harry was an only child and he was spoiled rotten. For that I take some responsibility: I gave him the impression that the world was his oyster, not knowing that he would try to take and take."

Mrs Mullins placed one of her wrinkled hands on her husband's arm. "Now, now."

Her spouse continued: "It is true. Despite our encouragement, we also enabled him more than we should have. Harry was a tyrant to others, yet we denied him nothing. He drank and gambled and was a villain through and through. We turned a blind eye and fed his schemes. He told me that he was going to clean up and open a shop here in town so that he could be nearby and help take care of us.

"I foolishly believed him. I gave him my life savings, accumulated from a meagre pension from injuries I suffered thirty-two years ago in the Crimean War back in 1858. Little did I know that he squandered that in just a few nights at a roulette

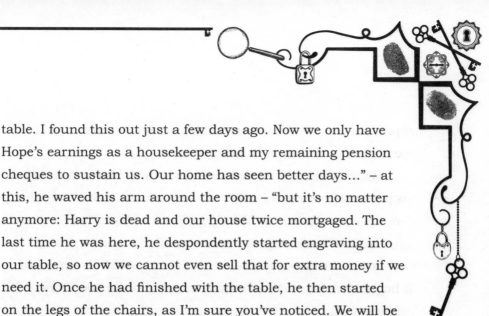

table. I found this out just a few days ago. Now we only have Hope's earnings as a housekeeper and my remaining pension cheques to sustain us. Our home has seen better days..." – at this, he waved his arm around the room – "but it's no matter anymore: Harry is dead and our house twice mortgaged. The last time he was here, he despondently started engraving into our table, so now we cannot even sell that for extra money if we need it. Once he had finished with the table, he then started on the legs of the chairs, as I'm sure you've noticed. We will be lucky to keep a roof over our heads in our old age." He got up and left the room to collect another log for the fire. Mrs Mullins offered to get us more tea, which we both accepted.

"Watson, there is something off about Joshua's story," said Holmes to me, quietly once we were alone. "Take a look at your chair's legs while I examine mine. Tell me if you find something. There must be a better reason for the table being carved and the chairs not being straight."

I did as my friend asked and, while his examination was fruitless, I found a cap on the end of one leg of my chair and a slip of paper inside. I quickly put it in my coat pocket and replaced the cap on the leg.

What has aroused Holmes's suspicions about Joshua's story?

"There is much to sort through," I agreed. "Why would he just hand over the pension he saved for thirty-two years? I can attest that it's not a large amount of money each month, but when saved for that long a period of time..."

"That's exactly it, Watson," said Holmes. He said he got his wound in the Crimean War back in 1858, but the fighting was over by early 1856. He either gave more to his son than he told

us, or Mullins didn't take everything after all, but Mr Mullins doesn't want Mrs Mullins to know that."

Mr and Mrs Mullins returned from their chores and we both received another cup of tea.

I continued: "Harry had a good job as a coachman and general handyman with the Bracewells."

"Yes, we thought it would be a turning point for him, and it might have been. But his sins caught up with him," Mrs Mullins said.

"Did you ever find out more from him about this 'M'?" Holmes asked.

"We did not," said Mrs Mullins. "But..."

"We ought to tell them," Mr Mullins said gently. "There can be no harm now."

He paused for a moment and studied his teacup. Holmes and I accepted his silence and sipped our tea. He continued: "Not very long ago, about a month, a young lad in his early twenties appeared at our door. He insisted that Harry had wronged him and his mother. Naturally, we were curious. Aside from paying his bills, we were never privy to the particulars of his life.

"This boy showed us a locket that contained a picture of our very own Harry and some strange symbols," he walked to the mantelpiece and showed us a slip of paper.

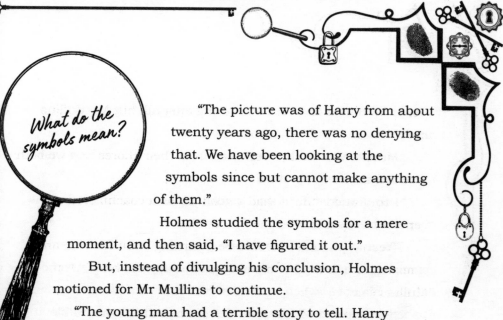

What do the symbols mean?

"The picture was of Harry from about twenty years ago, there was no denying that. We have been looking at the symbols since but cannot make anything of them."

Holmes studied the symbols for a mere moment, and then said, "I have figured it out."

But, instead of divulging his conclusion, Holmes motioned for Mr Mullins to continue.

"The young man had a terrible story to tell. Harry apparently ruined his mother – she was with child out of wedlock. Harry abandoned her and their child shortly after birth and she had to go to the workhouse. She eventually married a sympathetic soul and found a happy life. For years, the boy vowed revenge for the hardships his mother went through, and said he would have it."

"What did you do?" Holmes asked.

"I promised to write to Harry and offered to pay the lad what we had."

"I thought that Harry had taken your life savings and gambled it away?"

Mr Mullins looked at his wife and said, "You are very observant, Mr Holmes. I confess that I had a few years of pension hidden away. The pension was sent here to Hope, while I still served as best as I could in the Crimea, even after the war ended, as part of the security force – where I received a standard wage too. Records were poorly kept, so no one noticed that I was collecting both a wage and a pension. I had had to leave behind my young son and wife to fight and I wanted to provide for them as best as I could. I did so for a few years until my wound got

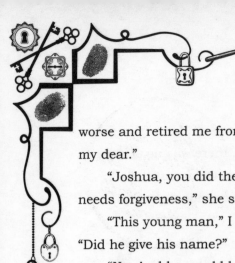

worse and retired me from service permanently. I'm sorry, my dear."

"Joshua, you did the best you could. You did nothing that needs forgiveness," she said.

"This young man," I said, returning us to our investigations. "Did he give his name?"

"No. And he would have none of our money. He was as courteous to us as circumstances permitted, but there was no denying his anger when we denied him Harry's address. His face flushed a deep red and he pounded his fist on this very table; it was then we saw the face of our child in his."

"Did he give any indication as to what he would deem reasonable revenge?"

"Not a hint of it, but it obviously wasn't based on money," Mrs Mullins answered. "Having just met our grandchild, we weren't ready for him to leave, but we could not convince him to stay. We tried to ask about his mother to see how she fared but he kept silent. We then wrote to Harry as promised, hoping he would solve this mystery for us."

"What was Harry's response?"

"He gave none and ignored our initial messages entirely," she said.

"Did you hear anything from him over the past few months?"

"Nothing beyond his plan to move here. That part of his story at least was true. We hoped to resume the conversation about his child once he lived near us."

"What do you think made Harry decide that moving to Kent would be sufficient to deter his creditors?"

"Oh, but he wasn't planning to stay," Mrs Mullins said.

"He was planning to head to South America. We were wondering how he was going to afford such a venture."

Where was Mullins getting the money to move to South America?

"I know how," said Holmes. "Your son was a very crafty – and manipulative – man."

"We have no money left," said Mr Mullins. "And, with his debts, he would have had to come into a great fortune to pay them off and to afford his move. I hope he wasn't planning anything nefarious."

"Your son's employer, Lord Bracewell, will have offered Harry the money," Holmes said. "We believe that this is the money that was found on him after he died."

"We know Lord Bracewell," said Mrs Mullins. "He has been a kind man and tried to be a good influence on Harry. He offered Harry a job shortly after Lady Bracewell died. We know that our son was good with the children... so there was still good in him, despite his other troubles."

Holmes had no further questions, so I intervened: "What do you plan to do now?"

"We have no plans other than to continue with life as best we can," Mrs Mullins said.

"There may be hope yet," Holmes suggested. "Your son was found with a small fortune upon him, which was given to him freely by Lord Bracewell. That money will be returned to you along with his personal effects."

"We aren't beggars," Mr Mullins said proudly.

"We know the both of you mean well," his wife interjected, "but we can't hope for, or take, more from others. That's all our Harry ever did. My husband's pension and my housekeeping wages should be sufficient to allow us to reach our old age."

"Then take the money and set up a small business as Harry might have done and help others when you can," I suggested. "You also have a grandchild to think about, in case he ever reaches out to you again."

Holmes and I finished our tea, thanked our hosts and got up from the table. Holmes reached down to get the napkin he dropped and stared a moment at a series of scratches in the table. While our hosts cleared away the dishes to the kitchen, he motioned for me to look at the scratches. I studied them for a moment.

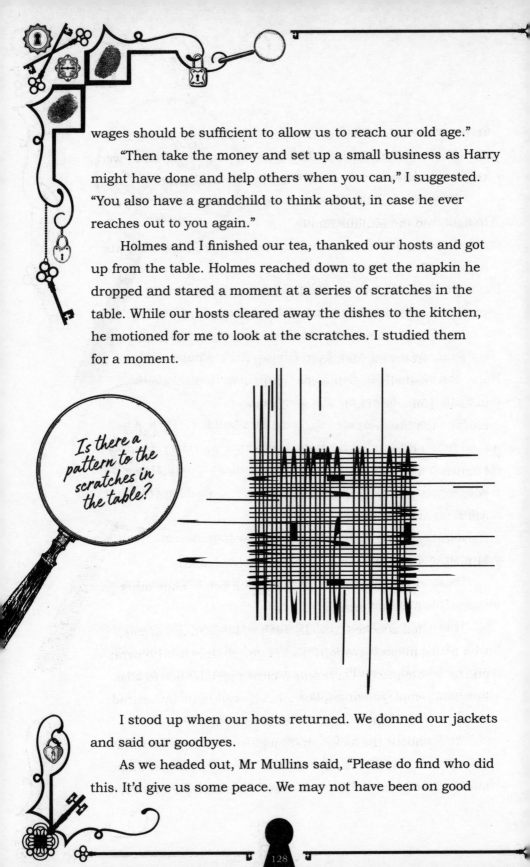

Is there a pattern to the scratches in the table?

I stood up when our hosts returned. We donned our jackets and said our goodbyes.

As we headed out, Mr Mullins said, "Please do find who did this. It'd give us some peace. We may not have been on good terms with our son, but nothing justifies his murder."

As we walked back to the station, I pondered, "What were those scratches in the table? They looked deliberate."

"They were deliberate, Watson. And this gives us more insight into the Mullins family."

"How can there be so many irreconcilable aspects to just one man?"

"They aren't irreconcilable. Harry Mullins showed each party what he wanted them to see," Holmes replied.

"And what do you make of this young boy? Should we not try to ascertain his identity?" I asked.

"I already have deduced who the boy is," said Holmes. "There are a number of clues to his identity."

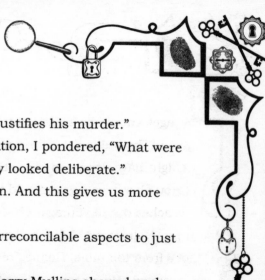

What is the identity of Mullins's child?

"What do you mean, Holmes?" I asked. "The only people we have met who fit the young man's description are servants at Westwood Manor, and they surely would have known where to find Mullins instead of needing to seek out his parents."

"Watson," said Holmes. "This young boy is none other than Miss Amelia Forman."

I was too shocked to walk further. I looked at Holmes, who asked in exasperation: "Didn't you notice the photographs on the mantelpiece? There was a clear resemblance to Miss Forman's employment application, showed to us by Lestrade. Or were you too preoccupied with the furniture?

"How about the locket that included Mullins's picture? Does that not appear similar in description to the one found on Mullins's body containing a picture of his fiancée? Finally, the

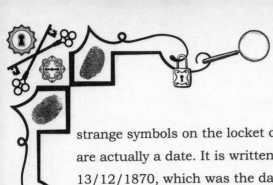

strange symbols on the locket containing Mullins's photograph are actually a date. It is written as a mirror image. The date is 13/12/1870, which was the day of Miss Forman's birth, I believe."

"Miss Amelia Forman is Mullins's daughter," I repeated dumbly, as I tried to get my head around this new fact. "But the diary?"

"Why," Holmes meditated rhetorically, "do we trust or mistrust the written word? They are simply words. There is no reason to assume that anything Miss Forman wrote, or anything she told us when we interviewed her, is factually true or untrue."

"You are assuming that she staged this encounter to murder her father?"

"I assume nothing of the kind. She accepted this position and it brought her closer to her father. He died. The events may be connected or not. We simply don't know."

"Do you suspect her?"

"I suspect the motives behind her diary. It's too much of a coincidence for Miss Forman to apply for, and get, a job that would bring her to the very man she has so much reason to despise. The diary is curiously unforthcoming about her motivation, unless she wrote it to throw us off the scent deliberately. The circumstances are suspicious and we would do well to interview Miss Forman once more, whether to prove her innocence or her guilt."

"And the papers I found in the hollowed-out leg of the chair?", I asked.

"We'll have time to review those shortly, my dear Watson. But for now, let us pay Mrs Kemp and Miss Forman a visit."

As we walked to the railway station, I reached into my

pocket and pulled out the slightly burned paper that I had found hidden in the chair leg.

"Well, Watson?" asked Holmes, "What does it say?"

I carefully smoothed out the paper. I could only read the last few lines. The rest had been burnt. It must have been extracted from the fire before flames had consumed it entirely.

> *I truly loved you once, Harry, and part of me will love you forev...*
> *...the pain is too much, and I must move on with my life. I have met...*
> *...lease never contact me again.*
>
> *...ve, always,*
> *...nina*

Now turn to page 54.

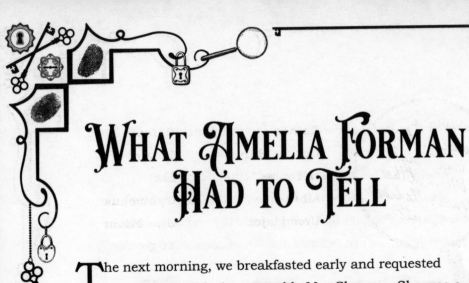

What Amelia Forman Had to Tell

The next morning, we breakfasted early and requested an interview with the venerable Mrs Clemens. She was a woman of around 45 who exuded dignity and self-possession, even in the face of such domestic woes as these. She answered all of our questions regarding the house staff – the number of whom had reduced since Lady Bracewell's death. She then led us to Charlie and Matilda's nursery, which was separated from the rest of the house by a labyrinth of stairs. Each landing was beset with a vase of flowers and greenery from the estate. As we were walking down the stairs, Holmes bent and picked up a small, crushed, purple wildflower from the otherwise immaculate floor and put it in his pocket.

The nursery itself was a cosy room. It looked like somewhere the children played often. The ceiling was covered with a painting of the night sky. I remarked on this to Mrs Clemens.

She smiled sadly and said: "The Bracewells were so happy to have children and felt especially blessed to have twins. Lord Bracewell used his connections with the nearby university to have a star chart of 12 December 1881 painted here to mark their date of birth. The family, of course, also used the constellations to navigate the seas for generations.

"He left off one constellation on purpose, saying that his family will always be connected to the stars, so they don't need to wait for St Elmo's Fire as a good omen."

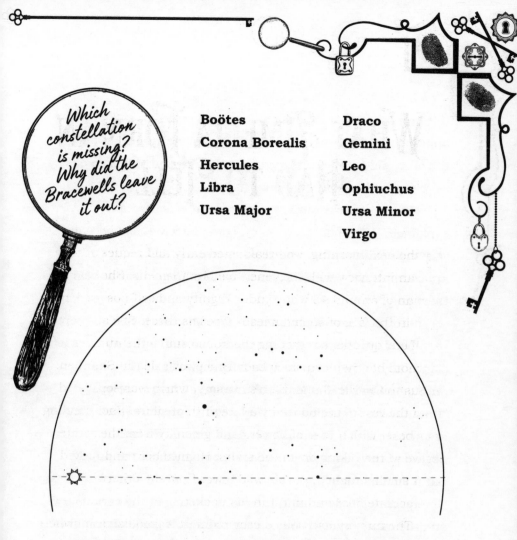

Which constellation is missing? Why did the Bracewells leave it out?

Boötes
Corona Borealis
Hercules
Libra
Ursa Major

Draco
Gemini
Leo
Ophiuchus
Ursa Minor
Virgo

I looked up at the sky on the ceiling to see if I could figure out what was missing, but I could not immediately determine what it was. Holmes, for his part, took no notice and it dawned upon me, as it had done before, that knowledge of the stars was entirely foreign to him.

As Holmes seemingly had no interest, I kept going over in my mind what could be missing from the room. After recalling my nights of stargazing, I was finally able to determine that the constellation Gemini, the twins, was missing. I smiled at my revelation, knowing that Castor and Pollux are the brightest stars in that constellation. When St Elmo's Fire appears in

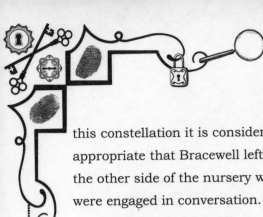

this constellation it is considered a good omen for sailors. How appropriate that Bracewell left off this constellation. I walked to the other side of the nursery where Holmes and Mrs Clemens were engaged in conversation.

"This room was until recently a kind of cellar," she explained. "In the past few years, Lord Bracewell has become very resistant to noise. The children are well-behaved, but they are children nevertheless, and he can no longer bear to hear them play."

"Did they have a governess before Miss Forman?"

"No. Lord Bracewell taught them himself, but they were left principally to their own devices during playtime. They want for nothing materially." She paused, before adding more gently: "It was I who suggested that they need a caregiver when they are not at school. The master is a good man, yet he has neglected their emotional needs. He bought them the puppy, but it isn't enough."

Holmes strode around the room, looking at the various toys and the many, many books on the shelves. A game of draughts sat on a small table and a pair of dice in a cup sat on the corner. He looked into the cup and saw a slip of paper, likely a set of directions.

"What do you make of this?" asked Holmes.

"Mullins was always playing games with the children. I wasn't fond of him teaching them how to play with the dice, but he promised that it was only instructional and not anything related to gambling. He was always teaching them new things to keep them occupied and out of trouble. They were so sad when he told them that he was leaving to take care of his parents. He said that if they felt sad after he left, they could play the games he taught them, especially the dice game, and they could remember the good times they had together."

Holmes unfolded the paper in the dice cup. To his astonishment, his name appeared on the paper, along with a diagram of two dice and a compass with the N circled and an arrow pointing down.

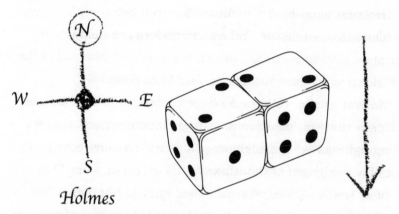

Holmes

"Dear woman," he cried. "Please at once tell me why my name is on this slip of paper? How could my name appear here before I was even brought in on this case?"

"Mr Holmes!" Mrs Clemens exclaimed, "I swear to you that this room has not been touched since the children disappeared. I do not know why your name is on that slip of paper. It was Mullins who played this game with them, I swear it!"

Holmes, visibly shaken, accepted her word and wrote down the entire message from the slip of paper in his journal. "This is very curious, Watson, and a puzzle to be solved another time."

Holmes walked around the room, taking note of the sheer number of books in the room. "The children are voracious readers?" he wondered.

Mrs Clemens smiled. "Very much so – just like their father."

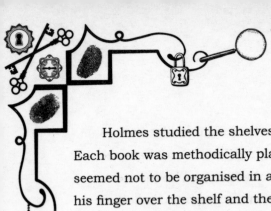

Holmes studied the shelves of books at considerable length. Each book was methodically placed. To me, though, they seemed not to be organised in any meaningful way. Holmes ran his finger over the shelf and there was not a speck of dust to be found. I heard a "Hrm..." come from him as he did so. Naturally, he said nothing, so I pressed him.

"Holmes, what have you found?"

"Only that, while the shelves themselves are immaculate, there is a series of peculiar lines etched into the rear wall of the shelf. Not a single line straight across. Thoughts?"

"At first glance, Holmes, I notice nothing. It is only on one shelf. Now that you mention it, though, it's rather odd that it isn't straight across the shelf, as you said. The only thing I can think of is the height of the books."

"Very well observed, Watson. Your eyes do not betray you. However, I'm assuming it was just their mother's way of showing them where the books were to be replaced after reading them."

"Is this playroom regularly cleaned?" he asked Mrs Clemens.

"We air it out every other day. But the children are very particular about the arrangement of the books, probably because the strongest memories they have of their mother are of her pulling the books down from the shelf and reading them stories," she replied. "We have left the room exactly as it was when the children disappeared."

"For that, I am very glad," said Holmes. He took one final stroll around the room, pausing

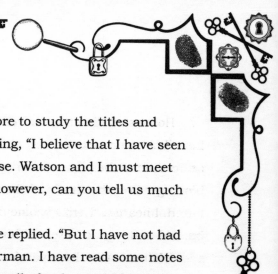

in front of the bookcase once more to study the titles and heights of the spines, before noting, "I believe that I have seen all that I need to see in this house. Watson and I must meet Miss Forman. Before we leave, however, can you tell us much about her?"

"I placed the ad myself," she replied. "But I have not had the pleasure of meeting Miss Forman. I have read some notes about her. But she was quite unwell after her ordeal so we thought it best to leave her with Mrs Kemp for now."

"Can we have Mrs Kemp's address – as well as the address for Mullins's parents?"

Mrs Clemens noted down both of them for us, explaining, as she handed us the information on Mullins's parents, that she only knew of the general vicinity where they lived. They had a small, but comfortable, cottage on a small road in Canterbury in the county of Kent, right near the cathedral. The exact street and cottage number, she did not know.

Holmes and I set out for Mrs Kemp's house, about three miles away from Westwood Manor. We were certain that the long walk would do us good and help to clear our minds. As we walked out of the Bracewells' home – this time by the south main gate – I breathed in the smell of the great outdoors and the moist earth, and pondered over the puzzles before us. The estate was in the full bloom of spring. The trees were thick with leaves and the gardens from which Mrs Clemens took the flowers that decorated the house were in full bloom. A lush carpet of grass blanketed the estate and horses grazed in pastures on the high sweet grasses and wildflowers. The silence was occasionally broken by chirping birds. How different this area was to our usual environment of central London!

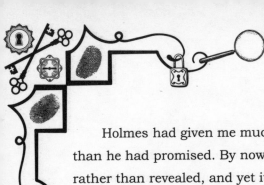

Holmes had given me much to think about and yet far less than he had promised. By now, I knew his ways: he tantalised rather than revealed, and yet it was clear that he had a plan of how the different threads of this mystery would converge.

Holmes was a brisk walker and it was all I could do to keep up. He spoke all the way, of Vivaldi and cricket and of tobacco and poison. Finally, I asked him about the affair at the Natural History Museum.

"Wright was murdered," said Holmes, "and he was complicit in the crime in some way. Perhaps he saw something, but my suspicion is that he was more directly involved. His anxiety following the burglary led me to suspect him. I also suspect he was not the only one responsible. I am closing in on this party: the two telegrams I sent revealed that there had been a burglary, but what was stolen was still seemingly accounted for.

"Remember the newspaper article? It is as if someone is taunting us, showing us a clue that is hidden in plain sight. Only someone with a great amount of influence could ensure that the spelling errors would remain in the newspaper article we read." At this point, he put his fingers on his lips. "A sportsman must not show his hand prematurely."

Following the rains over the previous days, the sun shone brightly, and the foliage bloomed and blossomed. It brought a certain liveliness to the morning. If there had not been so much at stake – the missing children, the murdered man, the broken father – it might even have been a pleasurable occasion to listen to my friend's deep knowledge of music.

After about an hour of walking, we reached Mrs Kemp's boarding-house. Upon our first glance, it appeared to be an

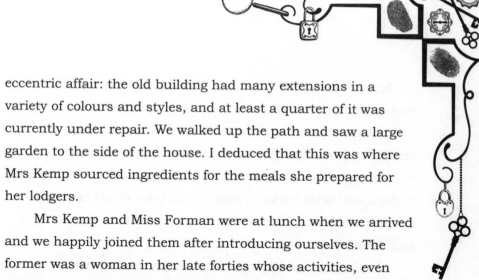

eccentric affair: the old building had many extensions in a variety of colours and styles, and at least a quarter of it was currently under repair. We walked up the path and saw a large garden to the side of the house. I deduced that this was where Mrs Kemp sourced ingredients for the meals she prepared for her lodgers.

Mrs Kemp and Miss Forman were at lunch when we arrived and we happily joined them after introducing ourselves. The former was a woman in her late forties whose activities, even at the table, belied her age. She was busily writing letters and dictating to a maid a forthcoming lecture on the importance of philanthropy in these times. The latter – what can I say? – was loveliness personified. The house, we were told, usually housed ten to twelve female lodgers, but it was currently vacant except for the hostess and the governess.

The house, while eccentric on the outside, was charming on the interior. A small sitting room with comfortable couches and a small table for tea sat surrounded by walls filled with books. The fresh smell of flowers lingered in the air. A gold candlestick moulded in the likeness of Psyche caught the light from the midday sun near the sitting area by the door that led to the kitchen. A small stairway led to the guest quarters, with a series of doors barely visible that were barricaded due to the ongoing reconstruction.

Mrs Kemp's sympathies for those in poor circumstance evidently aligned so closely with Hewitt's that he could not have chosen a better refuge for Miss Forman. Even on such a short acquaintance, Mrs Kemp had become visibly attached to, and protective of, her newfound friend. She took a break from dictation to fetch her young charge some tea. She added a tiny

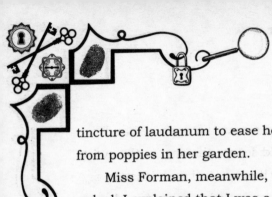

tincture of laudanum to ease her stress, cultivated no doubt from poppies in her garden.

Miss Forman, meanwhile, was still distraught over her ordeal. I explained that I was a medical doctor and asked to take her pulse and temperature. She was feverish, but the danger had passed. Miss Forman began to question us immediately.

"Mr Holmes, I have read your romance about poor Lucy and Jefferson."

"I am glad," he answered. Holmes may not have used such a term himself to describe the Jefferson affair, but I could see that he was privately happy that the account of his powers of reasoning had travelled widely.

"Be honest with me, Mr Holmes, have there been any new developments? Do you know where the children are? How is their father? Do you know who the murderer is? Why was the coachman killed?"

"I have answers to almost all of your questions, Miss Forman, but you must allow me to show my hand only when the time is ripe. I have come to ask you some questions."

"You have read my diary."

"I have, yes."

"Its contents were never meant to be shared."

"Whatever you wrote in it is safe with us. We want to hear your version of what happened after you left the station."

Mrs Kemp made a motion to intervene, but Miss Forman was determined to help: "I am happy to answer any questions you have." She began instantly to offer us information.

"Nothing eventful happened at the station after I found the children and Spot. It started to rain. The driver held an umbrella over us while we climbed into the carriage and then encouraged

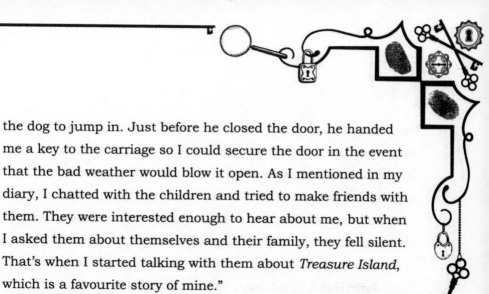

the dog to jump in. Just before he closed the door, he handed me a key to the carriage so I could secure the door in the event that the bad weather would blow it open. As I mentioned in my diary, I chatted with the children and tried to make friends with them. They were interested enough to hear about me, but when I asked them about themselves and their family, they fell silent. That's when I started talking with them about *Treasure Island*, which is a favourite story of mine."

"Very good. Now, why don't you take us back to the scene of the carriage?"

"I shall do my best."

"We know that the carriage stopped abruptly. How long was it between that event and the sound of the gunshot?"

"It must have been almost ten minutes. You see, Mr Holmes, I was writing and trying to reassure my pupils even as the events were unfolding. To calm their nerves, I asked them to tell me about the map in *Treasure Island* and about the locations on it."

"Yes, your account was very clear. Can you describe the sound you heard?"

"It was a loud thud and the carriage shook somewhat."

"Was it sharp?"

"I am not sure," she confessed. "I had no intention to fib in my diary, but I had to describe it somehow."

"Yes, of course. Did the sound startle the horses? Was there a jolt or were they neighing with fright?"

"No, the horses were not particularly agitated."

"What happened after you left the passenger seat?"

"I told the children to continue looking at the map. While they were distracted, I moved in front of them and secured my

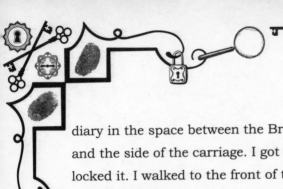

diary in the space between the Bracewell family coat of arms
and the side of the carriage. I got out, closed the door and
locked it. I walked to the front of the car where I saw the
coachman sitting still. I called out to him and, when he didn't
respond, I reached up and shook his leg. He slumped forward
and didn't move."

"Was there blood?"

"None that I could see. I climbed up into the seat next to
him to check on him, but he had no pulse."

"What did you do next?"

"I was shocked and wet. I could not help the poor man, so
I decided to stay with the children and wait out the storm with
them. I slipped on the wet wood and fell when I tried to get out
of the driver's seat, I hit my head against something hard and
must have been unconscious for a few minutes. I came to and
made my way back to the cabin. The winds beat against me and
the rains poured without inhibition. I could see, already, that
disaster had struck: I had asked the children to remain in the
carriage and keep the door closed, but when I returned, it was
blowing open in the wind. I looked for the key upon my person
and found it in the keyhole of the door, so someone must have
found it in my pocket while I was unconscious.

"When I got back into the cart, the children and the dog
were gone. All that remained was the copy of *Treasure Island*."

"Do you remember what page they were on?" Holmes asked.

"Yes, it was turned to the map. To keep them busy and
distracted, I had directed them to use the map to create a
narrative on how to get to four distinct places of their choosing."
She stepped away for a brief moment and returned with a note
that she handed to Holmes. It read:

We started east of the Foremast Hill and travelled south until we came to our third mountain range. Realising we'd gone entirely too far, we travelled northeast through a forest and came to a brief rest on the far side of a small hill, then southeast to Spring, settling in our final location.

Our second trip began where our first ended. We travelled west, back over the hill and through the forest. We decided to go southeast and stopped when we encountered a swamp. From there, southwest to where X marks the spot. We found no riches and so continued east until we tired.

The next trip began in the waters of the northeast. We travelled south for many miles before turning east and never looked back. Until we stopped of course.

Our final excursion began at Skeleton Island. We travelled north through White Rock all the way to the North Inlet. We changed from boat to hoof and went southwest to Spyeglass Hill. When we realised our folly, we went east and, from our perch at White Rock, spotted the boat we had travelled on sailing back to Skeleton Island.

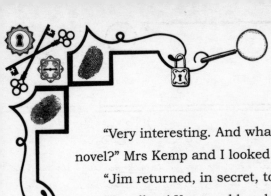

"Very interesting. And what point had they read up to in the novel?" Mrs Kemp and I looked at Holmes in wonder.

"Jim returned, in secret, to the Hispaniola."

"Excellent! You would make a fine detective if you put your mind to it, Miss Forman!"

We were too puzzled to respond to Holmes's compliment. He continued:

"What did you do next?"

"With the last of my strength, I closed the door and locked myself in with my key. I lost consciousness for the second time until I came around when I found myself here at Mrs Kemp's. I have a vague recollection of coming briefly to consciousness and seeing the face of another man, whom I now know to be George Hewitt, putting me in his carriage."

"What an honourable man," said Mrs Kemp. "He came knocking at my door and asked if he could bring up Miss Forman, as she had been involved in a nasty accident. I recognised him from his postal rounds, so I felt in safe hands with him as he has a position of trust in delivering the mail."

"I admit a bit of embarrassment," said Miss Forman. "I fear that I may have been mumbling in my unconscious state, but I didn't want to leave my diary behind in case something happened to me. I had a note for Anne in my last entry so my family would be taken care of in the event that I did not recover."

"You did the right thing, Miss Forman and your courage is formidable."

Miss Forman bowed. "Have you any further questions?"

"No more," Holmes replied. "But might I borrow your copy of *Treasure Island*?" Upon receiving Mrs Kemp's assent, he pulled the book off her bookshelf and looked at it for a few moments.

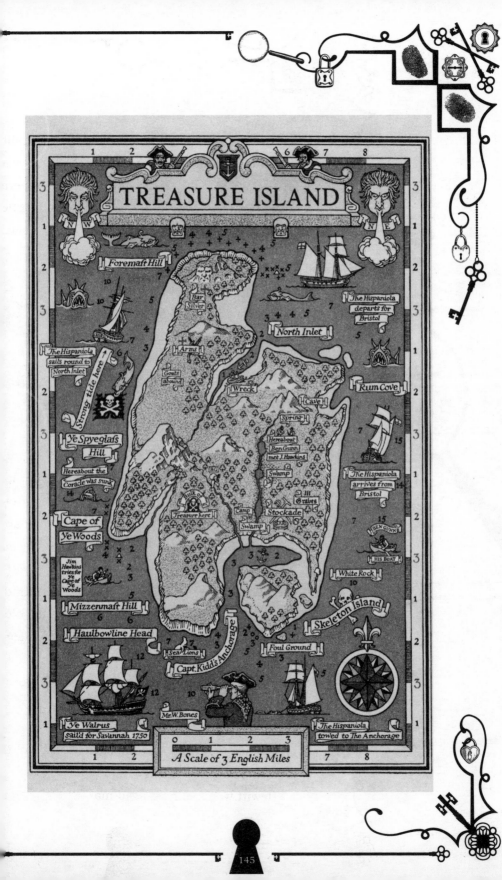

He looked at me and nodded and, without further ado, wished the two ladies a good morning. I followed him directly. We had not gone far before Holmes said to me: "At least one party is lying, Watson, but we will get to the bottom of it and recover the missing children. Do you recall the note Miss Forman handed me, the one the children wrote for her? I think it is no mere chance that they wrote what they did. If we plot the points they refer to on the map, what do you see?"

Using the map and the note, find out what the children really had to say.

Holmes handed me the book and I turned to the map and read the children's story again.

I followed the points on the map that they referenced. After looking at the map, I noticed a pattern emerging in the pathway. I started again from the beginning and eventually saw a word.

"Blimey," I said. "The children mapped out the word 'Help' before disappearing."

"But help for – or with – what?" pondered Holmes, "Or from whom? Perhaps we need a bit more background information on some of the characters in this tale.

"Watson, shall we speak to the Cromwell's employment agency for more information on Miss Forman and her background, or shall we visit Mullins's parents?"

If you would like to visit the Cromwell's employment agency, turn to page 88.

If you would like to visit Mullins's parents in Canterbury, turn to page 118.

The Net Is Drawn

"**A**ustralia?" I asked Holmes when we found ourselves outside Cromwell's after the arrest. "Why should we believe Miss Stoper now that we know she was complicit in the theft of the files? Bracewell – as you concluded – agreed to set her up in a business. Is she trying to throw us off track and cast doubt on her own crimes? If she is not lying, then who on Earth hosted us at Westwood Manor?"

"There is a definite connection between Lord Bracewell and Australia," said Holmes. "Bracewell spent the first half of his life there, which is no secret. Miss Stoper could be telling us a plausible lie to delay the investigation, since it would take a long time for a messenger to reach Australia to determine the truth of her statement. However, I believe I know the answer, which I will reveal once I am assured of my convictions. You can't judge a book by its cover, for it is the pages within that provide the true story."

This mysteriousness became almost too much for me to bear.

I began to demand that Holmes share his hunch, but suddenly one of his urchins came up to us and bowed deeply. He gave Holmes a telegram, which he tore open.

"Our nets are ready, my dear Watson.

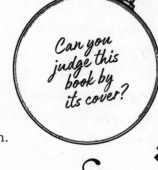

Can you judge this book by its cover?

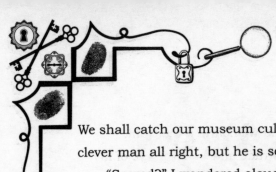

We shall catch our museum culprit before too long. He is a clever man all right, but he is scared."

"Scared?" I wondered aloud. "At least one man was killed."

"Yes, but all is not as it seems, Watson. The most dangerous force behind this mystery is one that we cannot see."

Holmes withdrew his pocketbook, scribbled a quick note in pencil and tore out the page. He gave it to the young boy with a sovereign: "Make sure that this goes to Mrs Hudson and no one else. Make sure you stay outside when you deliver it to her and do not antagonise her while you are there, or I shall find others to deliver my messages." The boy scowled but gave another bow and disappeared into the crowded streets.

"Watson, we must return to north London. Hurry along. Lestrade will be waiting for us at the station to return with us to Finchley. We must discuss with him the developments over the last day before we embark on the next steps in this investigation."

"Why are you involving Mrs Hudson?" I asked, while keeping up with the large strides of my companion. "Surely she should be kept out of harm's way."

"That is precisely what I am doing, Watson," said Holmes. "I've told her that we've been unavoidably delayed and that I would like her to take the tickets I purchased for tonight's symphony and enjoy an evening out. I also asked her to leave a note on our door with instructions to Gregson, should he arrive before we do."

We made our way to the railway station and waited for Lestrade to join us. "I shall double-check the doors on the carriage this time, to avoid having to prise ourselves out," I said dryly.

Lestrade arrived promptly and we boarded the train. I sat across from Holmes and Lestrade and held the eye of my companion. It had been a trying few days and my nerves simply could not handle more excitement. I was quite unwilling to follow my friend another step without greater transparency on his part. Holmes read me perfectly.

"Are you prepared to ask all the questions that have been piling up in your mind?"

"Yes, Holmes," I replied tersely. "I don't understand why you must keep everything so close to the chest."

"That is my nature, my dear Watson. I have been doing this for many years and have not had a partner to my investigations and adventures – until recently. But, to the matters at hand: I had an inkling from the start that the Bracewell we met could have been someone other than the true Lord Philip Bracewell. Miss Stoper's revelation brought clarity to this picture." Although I cannot be sure of my own facial expression when I heard this, if it was anything like that which appeared at the same moment on Lestrade's countenance it would have been a study in surprise bordering on astonishment.

Why does Holmes suspect that the person they met is not the real Lord Bracewell?

"Let me tell the story as I see it," Holmes said, fixing his cap. "Lord Bracewell, I think we will find, left England some months ago on extended business to Australia... perhaps something poised to threaten the family business that he has worked so hard to rebuild.

"He left not knowing how long he would be gone, allowing his children to be cared for by Mrs Clemens, Mullins and the rest of the servants, many of whom were replaced shortly after his departure. The children found a second father in Harry Mullins, a man they already knew. Once Mullins gave his notice to leave, a governess was to be hired to take his place.

"Let me pose several questions to you both so that you may see things the way I see them. What life-changing event has happened to Lord Bracewell in recent years? And how could that have affected his recent behaviour?"

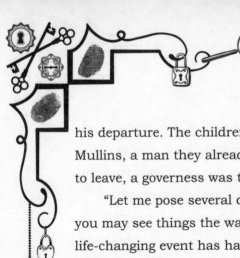

Can you answer the questions posed to Watson and Lestrade?

Lestrade and I stared blankly at each other before it dawned on me. "His wife, whom he loved dearly, passed away several years ago. I recall the staff saying he generally became a recluse after her passing and remained in his office."

"Precisely, Watson!"

I continued: "If that were me, I would not want to see anyone for some time. That would also explain why he suddenly found the sounds of the children playing hard to bear, and why the children found refuge in the lower level of the house."

"Now, many things were not quite as they should have been during our first visit to Westwood Manor," said Holmes.

"If you remember, when we were in the dining hall looking at the pictures of the past four generations of Lord Bracewells, I carefully studied the man whom we met shortly afterwards. He looked different, that is true, but ten years can change someone's appearance, especially after a series of tragedies. Lord Bracewell's father died, leaving him the dual responsibility of running the estate and the family business. Both have been in the family for generations, which would undoubtedly add extra pressure.

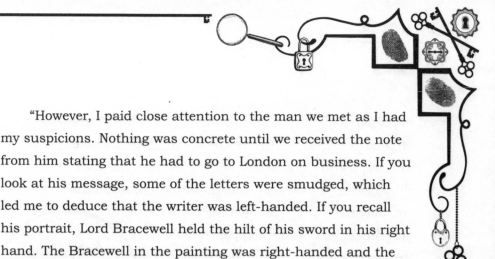

"However, I paid close attention to the man we met as I had my suspicions. Nothing was concrete until we received the note from him stating that he had to go to London on business. If you look at his message, some of the letters were smudged, which led me to deduce that the writer was left-handed. If you recall his portrait, Lord Bracewell held the hilt of his sword in his right hand. The Bracewell in the painting was right-handed and the Bracewell who we met was left-handed."

Lestrade and I looked at Holmes in shock, unable to believe what we were hearing.

"The fellow we have been dealing with is obviously his kinsman, a man of at least passing resemblance to the real thing," said Holmes.

"Surely, his neighbours and tenants must know Bracewell by sight," said Lestrade.

"And what about the household?" I added.

"I believe some members of the staff are involved. The impostor – let us refer to him as such – installed himself in the house shortly after the abrupt departure of the true Lord Bracewell. I would say that he left within the year. The children would certainly know that the man was not their father, but they made no mention of him when they met Miss Forman. It must be the case that the children do not know his identity, knowing him as only another caretaker of the estate.

"However, being smart children, they must know that something is awry, since they left Miss Forman a message within the map of *Treasure Island*. They were kept away from Lord Bracewell by Mrs Clemens and Harry Mullins. His plan, I think, was quite a masterful one. He could simply stay in the house and run the estate, living quite a comfortable life and

keeping the children under his control as unknowing hostages. They were none the wiser that they had been kidnapped and there was never any need to remove them, much less involve the police."

The train rattled on as Lestrade and I listened intently to Holmes unravel the threads of the mystery.

"The main question now is this, why did Mrs Clemens and Harry Mullins go along with this scheme? The imposter started replacing long-serving staff with new appointments, and this is where he needed the help of Miss Stoper. He offered her the money to start her own agency. Through her, he procured the services of Miss Forman, who would not know the impostor Lord Bracewell from the true one. She could operate as the children's immediate point of contact.

"However, as we know, nothing went according to plan. The coach was ambushed for an as yet unexplained reason, Mullins was killed and the children were kidnapped. Our impostor found himself in the tricky position of needing to recover the children whom he was trying to hide, or have his whole scheme revealed."

"Your theories, Mr Holmes, are rather fantastical. What is your evidence for all this?" interrupted Lestrade, as he removed a cigarette from his case, handing one to me also. Holmes lit our cigarettes before lighting his own pipe.

"I returned to central London, as Watson knows, with some inkling of what's what. A number of curiosities struck me from the beginning: it's true that Miss Forman's salary is inconsistent with her position, which would not necessarily lead her to question any peculiarities. The burglary at Cromwell's rather confirmed my suspicions, as what could anyone want with Miss Stoper's records?"

"You suspect that the impostor Lord Bracewell broke into the agency?" I asked, as I looked out of the window at the moving landscape.

"I am relatively sure of it. He has been missing since yesterday. When the eminently thorough Miss Stoper investigated Lord Bracewell's background to determine the type of client he would be, she discovered that the real Lord is in Australia. Her letter to the imposter may then have blackmailed him into setting her up with her own agency under the threat of her revealing his identity. He had no choice but to agree. Why else would he give such a substantial sum of money to someone he had never met? Doubtless, he is trying to get rid of the files as we speak – which he stole to get back at his blackmailer – while also setting up Miss Stoper in business. Without evidence to the contrary, it looks like Miss Stoper resented Cromwell's decision to retire, so sabotaged the agency."

"But this does not even come close to solving the murder of Harry Mullins and the children's kidnapping," I said. "Are these crimes independent of each other, or are they related to our impostor?"

"There is one other person we've met who I would suspect could be a primary actor in this play," Holmes said. "And there is a very small detail that leads me to believe this to be the case."

"Holmes," Lestrade said. "There are many facts of this case that we have not yet investigated fully. Are you speaking in terms of an accusation, or do you simply have a suspicion?"

I waited for Holmes to answer, knowing

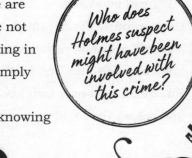

Who does Holmes suspect might have been involved with this crime?

that this could be a substantial revelation.

"I suspect Mr Hewitt," Holmes said. "It is a leap of logic, but I have my reasons."

My expectations were not disappointed.

"Now, see here, Holmes," said Lestrade. "Hewitt is the hero of this story! He rescued Miss Forman and made sure that she got help to recover from her injury. He is also a postman – that's an honourable position – and he has never, to our knowledge, committed a crime. He has been interviewed repeatedly and his story has not changed a jot. Can someone go from being a law-abiding citizen to a cruel murderer in the blink of an eye?"

"Let me draw the crime scene," Holmes started to explain. "I suspect that, for whatever reason, Hewitt had killed Mullins earlier in the day, and it was he who was driving the coach containing Miss Forman and the children. At a certain point in the trip, he stopped and staged the scene that Miss Forman described in her diary."

"But why?" asked Lestrade.

"Hewitt never meant to harm Miss Forman. In fact, his kindness towards her would distract us from his possible involvement in the other aspects at play. As, indeed, would the incorporation of something strange and incongruous like a corpse with a dry coat despite the torrential downpour outside, for example.

"You must also understand that this evidence is not entirely corroborated: Miss Forman never saw a carriage behind hers and she does not, or cannot, describe Hewitt or the driver who helped her and the children into the cab at the railway station. She mentioned only that his face was covered by his cap and collar. The children gave no indication of knowing or not

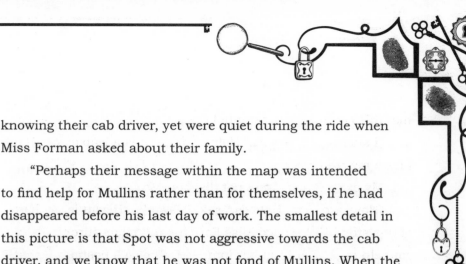

knowing their cab driver, yet were quiet during the ride when
Miss Forman asked about their family.

"Perhaps their message within the map was intended
to find help for Mullins rather than for themselves, if he had
disappeared before his last day of work. The smallest detail in
this picture is that Spot was not aggressive towards the cab
driver, and we know that he was not fond of Mullins. When the
driver went to put Spot into the carriage, he was able to pet him
without difficulty. This leads me to believe that Spot knew who
Hewitt was, as he is the postman who regularly delivers mail to
the estate. Hewitt had the means and an opportunity to commit
this crime. We must now find out if he also had a motive."

"If what you are saying is true, Holmes, then where are the
children now?" I wondered.

"I have a very good idea of where they are, but I want us to
play this game by my rules."

"How do you mean?" asked Lestrade, knitting his brows.

"I want to recruit some help."

"Whom do you wish to recruit?" I asked, confused.

"Impostor Bracewell."

Lestrade and I started.

"I thought we were going to arrest him!" The inspector cried.

"He is in a unique position to help us." Holmes continued.

"How do you mean?" I asked.

"You see, Hewitt does not know that Lord Bracewell isn't the
real Bracewell. We can use that to our advantage."

Try as we might, we could get no more details from Holmes.
We arrived at Finchley station and made our way to Westwood
Manor. When we arrived, the same footman we had seen before
took us to the study to meet with the man purporting to be Lord

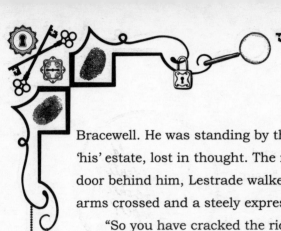

Bracewell. He was standing by the roaring fire, looking out upon 'his' estate, lost in thought. The moment the footman closed the door behind him, Lestrade walked straight up to our host with arms crossed and a steely expression that invited confrontation.

"So you have cracked the riddle, Mr Holmes," Bracewell said calmly, though his ashen face betrayed his surprise at this ambush. "You will know too, then, that I have yet to do anything wrong. I did not, and would not, kidnap the children."

"You are quite right. We cannot yet arrest you for your schemes," Holmes replied. "However, we can arrest you for the robbery at Cromwell's."

"And what, exactly, am I supposed to have stolen?" asked the impostor Lord Bracewell. "Search the house. You will find no evidence of theft of any sort."

What does Holmes suspect the impostor Lord Bracewell has done with the files?

"We will momentarily," said Holmes.

"By all means," said Bracewell. "Let me lead you to wherever you would like to begin."

"That is not necessary, whoever you are," said Holmes. "It is unlikely that you would leave the stolen property in the house where it could be discovered. However, that is quite a large fire for the middle of May. Watson, I wonder if files make good kindling?"

"More baseless accusations," said the impostor with a smile, as he glanced at the fireplace.

"Perhaps," my friend said. "Watson, check the fireplace for me, if you please."

I investigated the crackling fire and its surrounds. There were several scraps of paper remaining in the corners of the fireplace. The scraps contained a 'C' on one and a partially

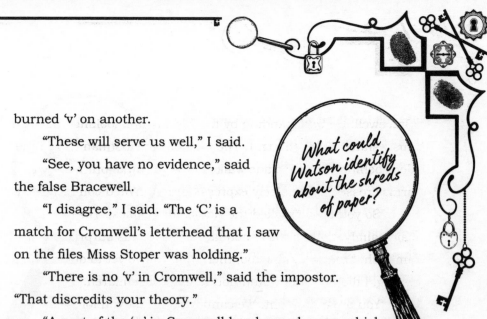

burned 'v' on another.

"These will serve us well," I said.

"See, you have no evidence," said the false Bracewell.

"I disagree," I said. "The 'C' is a match for Cromwell's letterhead that I saw on the files Miss Stoper was holding."

"There is no 'v' in Cromwell," said the impostor. "That discredits your theory."

"A part of the 'w' in Cromwell has burned away, which makes it look like a 'v'," I said.

Lestrade took the slips of charred paper and put them in his pocket to preserve the evidence.

"We require your help," said Holmes.

It was now the impostor's turn to be surprised.

"Help?" he repeated.

"Surely you don't want any harm to come to the children?" said Holmes. "Unless I am strongly mistaken, they are your kin in some regard. You can help us recover them. Perhaps a drink will calm your nerves.

As if we were at home in Baker Street, Holmes walked slowly to a large globe with a line running around the middle. While maintaining eye contact with our impostor friend, he rotated the globe, reached down and pressed something on it. We heard a click. Holmes flipped up the globe's northern hemisphere, removed a decanter and a few glasses from it and poured us each a drink. He handed us our glasses and I made sure to notice which hand Bracewell used to take it from him.

Sure enough, as our impostor gripped his glass tightly in his left hand, I wondered how Holmes knew the globe housed a

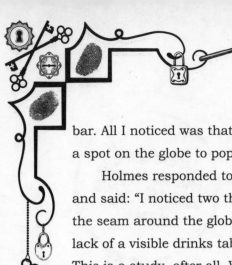

bar. All I noticed was that he touched
a spot on the globe to pop it open.

How did Holmes know that the globe would open, and how to open it?

Holmes responded to my glare
and said: "I noticed two things here:
the seam around the globe, and the
lack of a visible drinks table in the room.
This is a study, after all. With Bracewell's
connections to global travel and the globe being the
right size to house a decanter, I took an educated
guess by pressing the continent of Australia."
Turning to the impostor, he asked, "Would you like to
tell us your story?"

"I am Peter Brooks," he said. "I have as much claim to this
estate as Philip Bracewell himself. His grandfather disowned my
mother, Florence, when she eloped, and as such, I have always
known poverty. I don't hold it against my cousin: he is, by all
accounts from others I've met, a good man.

"I made inquiries about him after hearing of the death of
his wife. I was shocked when I first saw him, it was as if I was
looking into an improperly set mirror. The resemblance between
the two of us is uncanny. He heard of a threat to the business
from his Australian office and understood that it would take him
away for an extended period.

"I began investigating the servants at Westwood Manor.
I approached Harry Mullins first. I followed him to a pub and
offered to pay off some of his debts if he supported me in
assuming Philip's identity and running the estate. We sealed
our agreement with me promising to give him Philip's engraved
cigarette case. I had thought at first to keep this as 'proof' of
my identity as we share initials. Between the two of us, we

convinced Mrs Clemens to follow our lead by establishing a
secret pension for her further down the line. All was going well,
until Mullins unexpectedly quit his position, and we needed
someone to take care of my young cousins. I decided that a
governess would be our best option and asked Mrs Clemens
to take care of the details.

"However, Miss Stoper discovered that I wasn't Philip
Bracewell and threatened to reveal this to the authorities. I once
again offered money from the Bracewell pot, and agreed to fund
her new agency. That way, I would at least be able to hire staff
who would know me as the true Lord Bracewell. Then, of course,
Mullins was murdered, the children were taken and you showed
up at my door."

"How did you expect to get away with this once the real
Lord Bracewell returned?" asked Holmes.

"My mother told me that this house is a part of my heritage,
and that the grandfather clock on the ground floor holds the
key. I was hoping to find something there that would give me my
share of this estate, at which point I would reveal my identity
to my cousin Philip. I've searched the clock thoroughly and
have not yet found the key. My only satisfaction is that the
confounded clock doesn't appear to be working, which does
cover up my heavy-handedness during my search."

"It is time to recover the children," said Holmes, bringing us
back to the matter in hand. "Are you willing to aid us in finding
your cousins? All we know is that they were last seen in a locked
carriage. I can see two options. The first is that they were taken
and are being held against their will; the second is that they are
missing and do not believe that they are in any danger."

"Mr Holmes, I am willing to help you on the condition that

you drop your investigation into the household," said Brooks. "I take full responsibility for any harm that the staff have caused under my direction. I may have made some poor decisions, but I am not such a bad man. Tell me what you want done and I will do it."

"You have a decision to make," Holmes said. "You can join us in the search for your cousins, or you can remain here. If they are found, you can continue as their caretaker. Alternatively, if a ransom note arrives for them, you can continue to act as Lord Bracewell and secure their release."

"Let us go," Holmes said to me. "And perhaps we will meet Miss Forman along the way, resolve her previous testimony and bring this case to some sort of a conclusion."

If you believe that the children were kidnapped and are being held against their will, turn to page 72.

If you believe that the children are missing, but in no immediate danger, turn to page 161.

EXTRACT FROM AMELIA FORMAN'S STATEMENT

Thus far, I have pieced together the story from my recollections – with the occasional nudge from Holmes, who is far more forthcoming with criticism than with praise – and from sources such as telegrams, newspapers and diaries. The time is ripe, however, to hand over this narrative entirely to a different storyteller and it will imminently become apparent why. This was left for us by Miss Forman.

My Statement: Amelia Forman, ███████████

It will surprise you, Sherlock Holmes, to read this letter from me. You may have surmised all or part of what I have to say, but I wouldn't want you to be misled in terms of what I did and did not do. What you read in my diary was entirely correct: it is true that I was the oldest child in a family where we often went to bed hungry, but that all changed when I was still very young.

When my mother married my stepfather, our family expanded when they had children of their

What is the date of the statement?

own. We were happy for many years until he passed away. It was at that time that I learned about my true father: a man who left my poor mother shortly after my birth. My mother would tell me nothing else, saying it was in the past and is best forgotten. In order to help my mother and stepsiblings, I sought work. When I approached Cromwell's, I was immediately placed with a family for a short period. When the family moved to France permanently, I returned to Cromwell's with more experience. It is also true that I was offered and accepted a position that was better than anything I could have expected.

You were quite right to ask what happened after I stopped writing in my diary. To remind you of what occurred, I had just shushed the children and had given them a puzzle to work on. I completed my diary entry, steeled myself and unlocked the carriage door. I locked the door again to protect the children. This is the point at which my falsehood began.

The rain was pouring down. I paused outside the door to survey my surroundings. I did not know what I was walking into, but I was determined to discover what was keeping us waiting. I heard a noise from the trunk at the rear of the carriage. I stepped back to see more of the scene, and found our driver struggling to remove another man's body from the rear of the carriage. He looked at me expectantly.

I have never been squeamish, and I think my lack of fear startled the man. Conversely, his calmness reassured me, and I was quite certain that he would harm neither me nor the children.

"I did not expect you to leave the carriage and

the children unattended, Miss."

"I left to ensure their safety. They are safely locked inside. Is he hurt?" I asked, nodding to the body.

"He is quite dead, and has been for hours," he told me. "The Devil has gained another monster."

We could barely hear each other over the rain. He directed me to a carriage, parked not far behind ours. I followed him, he opened the door and I climbed in. When we sat across from each other, he lit a cigar with trembling hands.

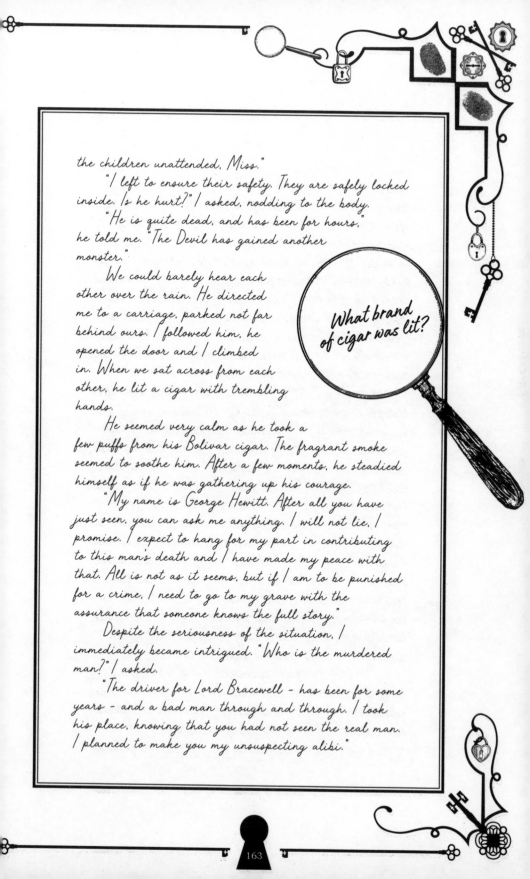

What brand of cigar was lit?

He seemed very calm as he took a few puffs from his Bolivar cigar. The fragrant smoke seemed to soothe him. After a few moments, he steadied himself as if he was gathering up his courage.

"My name is George Hewitt. After all you have just seen, you can ask me anything. I will not lie, I promise. I expect to hang for my part in contributing to this man's death and I have made my peace with that. All is not as it seems, but if I am to be punished for a crime, I need to go to my grave with the assurance that someone knows the full story."

Despite the seriousness of the situation, I immediately became intrigued. "Who is the murdered man?" I asked.

"The driver for Lord Bracewell - has been for some years - and a bad man through and through. I took his place, knowing that you had not seen the real man. I planned to make you my unsuspecting alibi."

"But why?"

"I wanted him dead, but I needed to make his death look accidental. Lord Bracewell is a good man, and for many years my family were his family's caretakers, but for the last two generations we have simply been his tenants. My grandfather had a disagreement with his grandfather - Lord Edward Bracewell - and we lost our status and position. My father lost his connection with Cecil Bracewell when he fled to Australia. It is only with the current Lord Bracewell that my family has somewhat re-established our ancestral connection as caretakers of the estate." George twisted a large signet ring with a stylised 'H' around his finger.

"However, Philip Bracewell entrusted far too much responsibility to Mullins, including the collection of rent from is tenants. The scoundrel abused his powers in every conceivable way. He extorted money and stole from us, seemingly with Bracewell's blessing, and there was nothing we could do. I tried to go to Westwood Manor and reason with Bracewell himself, but was denied an appointment with him. Apparently, we were to deal with his henchman alone. I tried to reason with him one night after a game down at the local pub. He drunkenly laughed in my face and told me I wouldn't have to deal with him for much longer because, since I was late with my rent, I would lose my home.

"I was never good with blood, but my hand was being forced. I knew his ways - everybody did - so I tracked him down at the local tavern last night. I discovered that he owed a lot of money to a nefarious man - I dare not even speak his name. This gave me

an idea of how to get rid of him and escape notice. I drugged his drink with a concoction supplied by a friend. Buying drugs at an apothecary would have left too much of a trail."

I thought for a moment and then the answer hit me.

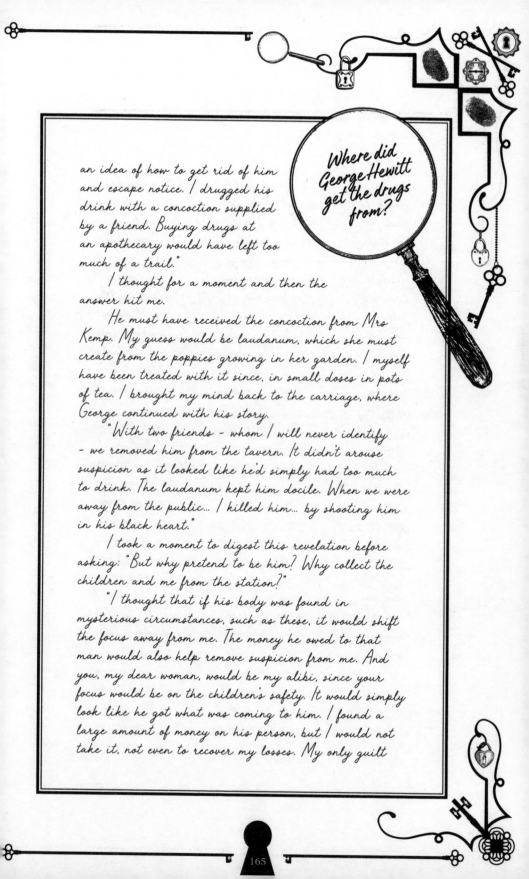

Where did George Hewitt get the drugs from?

He must have received the concoction from Mrs Kemp. My guess would be laudanum, which she must create from the poppies growing in her garden. I myself have been treated with it since, in small doses in pots of tea. I brought my mind back to the carriage, where George continued with his story.

"With two friends - whom I will never identify - we removed him from the tavern. It didn't arouse suspicion as it looked like he'd simply had too much to drink. The laudanum kept him docile. When we were away from the public... I killed him... by shooting him in his black heart."

I took a moment to digest this revelation before asking: "But why pretend to be him? Why collect the children and me from the station?"

"I thought that if his body was found in mysterious circumstances, such as these, it would shift the focus away from me. The money he owed to that man would also help remove suspicion from me. And you, my dear woman, would be my alibi, since your focus would be on the children's safety. It would simply look like he got what was coming to him. I found a large amount of money on his person, but I would not take it, not even to recover my losses. My only guilt

is regarding his lady, since she will never know what happened to him in his last moments."

"He had a lady?" I asked.

George handed over a locket. "I found this on his person."

I opened the locket and stared in shock at the portrait I saw inside. My hands started to tremble.

"What is wrong?" exclaimed George. He reached out and held my shaking hands.

"This picture is of my mother," I said, stuttering. "This means that... this horrible man that you describe... he must be my father!"

"Your father is Harry Mullins?" I could see a flicker of guilt pass his face, mixed with panic, as he realised that he had just confessed a murder to none other than the victim's kin.

The shock began to wear off and I collected myself. "I never knew him, or even saw him in person – until today. I agree with you that he was an evil man. He left my mother to raise me on her own, forcing her to work in horrible conditions for years until she met my stepfather." I looked George Hewitt directly in the eyes when I said: "He got what he deserved. But what do you intend to do now?"

George looked relieved at my words and said, "Nothing changes. You must return to the carriage and pretend that you never saw me. Do you promise?"

"I do, but perhaps I can help you." The man now had my full sympathies. Despite the shock of discovering my family connection to the corpse in the trunk of the carriage, I felt nothing for him. I, too,

had known my share of exploitative landlords and I understood George's motivations.

"How do you intend to help?" he asked.

"What if the children were to disappear temporarily? Then the investigation would shift towards their safe recovery," I said, my mind racing.

"I wish the children no harm," said George. "They are innocent in all of this."

"And neither do I. But what if we hid them in the house? In Westwood Manor? No one would be any the wiser. It might buy you some time to escape. You can flee to safety and then let the police know where the children are."

His eyes brightened in excitement: "I know exactly where in the house we can hide them, and I know who can help us."

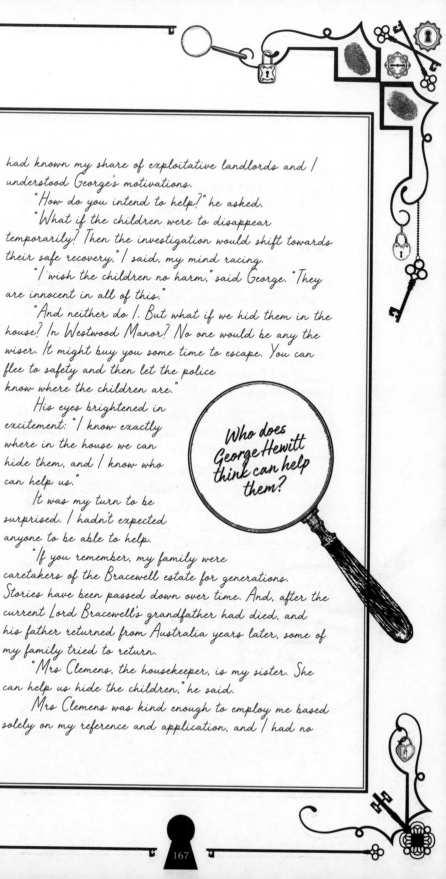

Who does George Hewitt think can help them?

It was my turn to be surprised. I hadn't expected anyone to be able to help.

"If you remember, my family were caretakers of the Bracewell estate for generations. Stories have been passed down over time. And, after the current Lord Bracewell's grandfather had died, and his father returned from Australia years later, some of my family tried to return.

"Mrs Clemens, the housekeeper, is my sister. She can help us hide the children," he said.

Mrs Clemens was kind enough to employ me based solely on my reference and application, and I had no

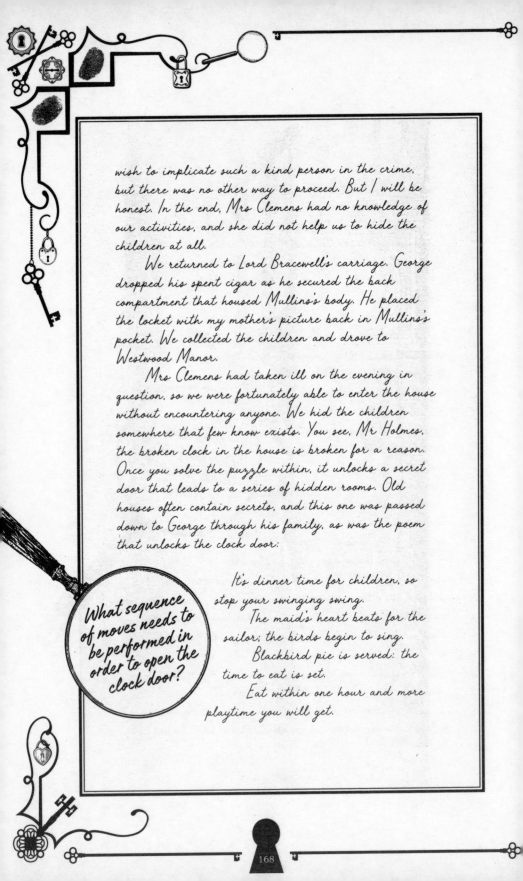

wish to implicate such a kind person in the crime, but there was no other way to proceed. But I will be honest. In the end, Mrs Clemens had no knowledge of our activities, and she did not help us to hide the children at all.

We returned to Lord Bracewell's carriage. George dropped his spent cigar as he secured the back compartment that housed Mullins's body. He placed the locket with my mother's picture back in Mullins's pocket. We collected the children and drove to Westwood Manor.

Mrs Clemens had taken ill on the evening in question, so we were fortunately able to enter the house without encountering anyone. We hid the children somewhere that few know exists. You see, Mr Holmes, the broken clock in the house is broken for a reason. Once you solve the puzzle within, it unlocks a secret door that leads to a series of hidden rooms. Old houses often contain secrets, and this one was passed down to George through his family, as was the poem that unlocks the clock door:

What sequence of moves needs to be performed in order to open the clock door?

It's dinner time for children, so stop your swinging swing.

The maid's heart beats for the sailor; the birds begin to sing.

Blackbird pie is served: the time to eat is set.

Eat within one hour and more playtime you will get.

I had told the children that we were to play a game, and they were delighted to find out about this secret inside their own house. We brought them there with plenty to eat and drink and locked the old clock door. I wagered that your attention, Mr Holmes, would be directed anywhere but in the house itself when you came to investigate their disappearance.

With the children taken care of, we returned to the carriage and drove back to where we had stopped, to stage the scene. We found our exact spot as the cigar butt was still in the mud. The question then was, how do we get Mullins's body into the driver's seat?

How did they stage the crime?

The rain made everything more difficult and the mud made movement treacherous. George lifted the body from the rear compartment of the carriage, hoisted it over his shoulder and walked to the front. We looped the rope from the side of the carriage around the body, under his arms, then pulled the rope through the iron ring near the driver's seat. George pulled the rope of our makeshift hoist, and as Mullins's body moved upwards, I directed it into the driver's seat.

At one point, George slipped in the mud and his hands flew against the carriage where he stabilised himself. His large ring rotated and scratched the side of the carriage. Mullins's body then slammed into my head and I saw stars. Feeling dizzy, I held the rope steady. Once he was back on his feet, George climbed into the driver's seat and moved Mullins's body so

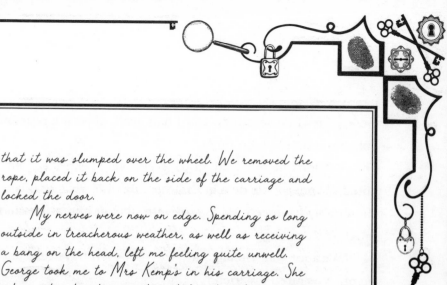

that it was slumped over the wheel. We removed the rope, placed it back on the side of the carriage and locked the door.

My nerves were now on edge. Spending so long outside in treacherous weather, as well as receiving a bang on the head, left me feeling quite unwell. George took me to Mrs Kemp's in his carriage. She administered a homemade sedative to calm my nerves and help with the dizziness. George left for the police station soon afterwards, to make his report.

As for me, I have become far too involved in this crime not to be considered an accessory, especially now that my parentage has been uncovered. I must make my departure, as George recently made his. Rest assured, my family knows nothing about my activities: who could have predicted that taking this job would culminate in my infamy? But if you had seen the look of desperation on George's face, I am sure you would have behaved in much the same way.

I do hope that we meet again and in better circumstances.

Amelia Forman

After he had finished reading Amelia's statement, Holmes smoked his pipe for some time.

"I was wrong," he said at last. "I had been thinking of the case in terms of corroboration. That is, I had looked for the commonalities and differences between Miss Forman's and

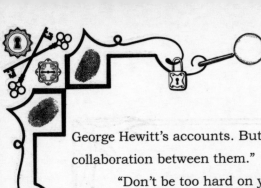

George Hewitt's accounts. But I had overlooked the possibility of collaboration between them."

"Don't be too hard on yourself," said Lestrade, who could ill conceal his delight that his ally-cum-rival had been so thoroughly trounced. He played with his hat and at last hid his laugh with a cough.

"Without you, Holmes, we wouldn't even have reached this point," I assured my friend.

Back at Westwood Manor, we found Mrs Clemens and told her what happened. She took us to the clock, whereupon following the instructions in the poem, we found the secret rooms:

It's dinner time for children, so stop your swinging swing. First, we held the pendulum still.

The maid's heart beats for the sailor; the birds begin to sing. Next, we pressed the heart-shaped rock on which the maid stood, and sure enough, the birds above her head started chirping, their mechanical beaks moving with the song.

Blackbird pie is served: the time to eat is set. Four and twenty blackbirds are baked in a pie, so we set the clock to twenty past four.

Eat within one hour and more playtime you will get. We simply added one hour, changing the clockface to twenty past five.

We recovered not only the children, but also a message. To put it more accurately, the children had found this document in one of the many chests in the secret rooms, and had already spent time decoding the message inside. This document, authored by the present Lord Bracewell's grandfather, was a surprise that none of us expected:

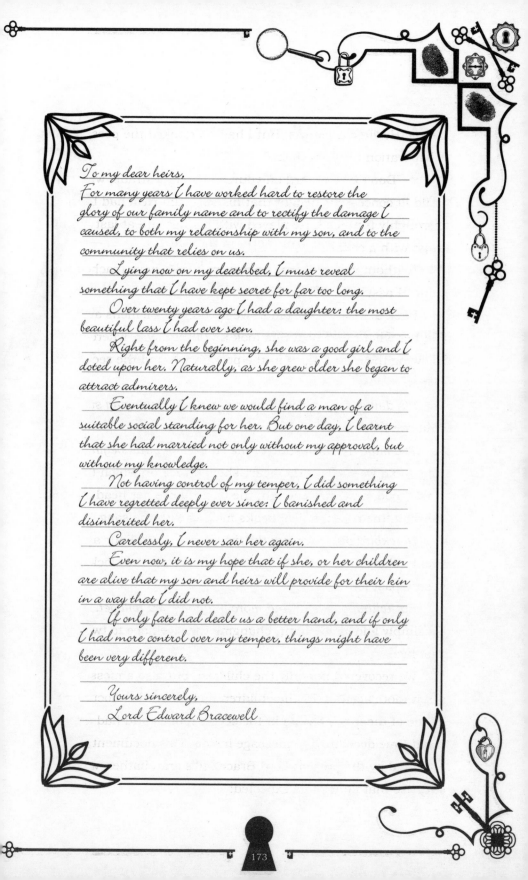

To my dear heirs,

For many years I have worked hard to restore the glory of our family name and to rectify the damage I caused, to both my relationship with my son, and to the community that relies on us.

Lying now on my deathbed, I must reveal something that I have kept secret for far too long.

Over twenty years ago I had a daughter: the most beautiful lass I had ever seen.

Right from the beginning, she was a good girl and I doted upon her. Naturally, as she grew older she began to attract admirers.

Eventually I knew we would find a man of a suitable social standing for her. But one day, I learnt that she had married not only without my approval, but without my knowledge.

Not having control of my temper, I did something I have regretted deeply ever since: I banished and disinherited her.

Carelessly, I never saw her again.

Even now, it is my hope that if she, or her children are alive that my son and heirs will provide for their kin in a way that I did not.

If only fate had dealt us a better hand, and if only I had more control over my temper, things might have been very different.

Yours sincerely,
Lord Edward Bracewell

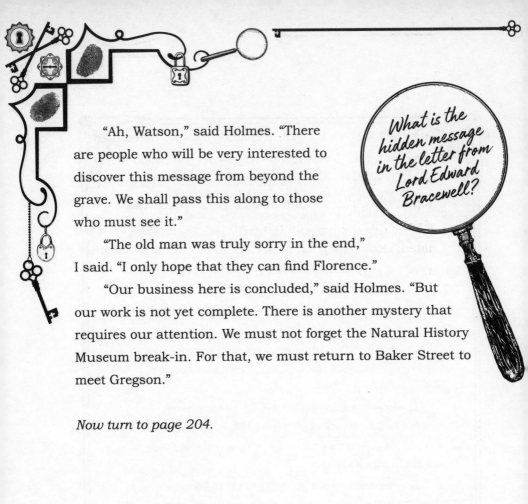

"Ah, Watson," said Holmes. "There are people who will be very interested to discover this message from beyond the grave. We shall pass this along to those who must see it."

"The old man was truly sorry in the end," I said. "I only hope that they can find Florence."

"Our business here is concluded," said Holmes. "But our work is not yet complete. There is another mystery that requires our attention. We must not forget the Natural History Museum break-in. For that, we must return to Baker Street to meet Gregson."

Now turn to page 204.

What is the hidden message in the letter from Lord Edward Bracewell?

"Let us start with Bracewell," replied Holmes. "He can tell us about the man Mullins and, on the way to Westwood Manor, we can examine the remnants of the crime scene. Afterwards, we can stop at the police station and examine the carriage. Time is of value, Watson, we do not wish the scene to be further contaminated." Holmes hailed a carriage and gave directions to the driver.

Now turn to page 16.

George Hewitt lived in an unattractive locality. Our cab brought us to a dingy street and we made our way from dark alley to dark alley in search of his home. Rats crawled through refuse strewn on the ground as stray dogs growled and barked at passers-by. The address Lestrade gave us was almost useless as the rain had caused the ink to run.

What is George Hewitt's address?

None of the doors were numbered. There was not a sign to be seen nor a neighbour to ask. Holmes and I wandered around, before returning to a door with an overhang where we could study the wet address more closely out of the rain.

"Ah," said Holmes, "I've finally got it. Hewitt lives at 136 Laurel Way, which should be somewhere around here.

We made our way down the street but could not find a door marked 136. Holmes spied a door down an alleyway with mail protruding from the letterbox.

"Wouldn't it be remarkable if the only door with visible mail were to be the one belonging to our postman?"

"Indeed, Holmes!"

Holmes knocked. And knocked. At length, the postman, eyes heavy with sleep, opened his door.

Hewitt was a middle-aged man with thick sideburns and a

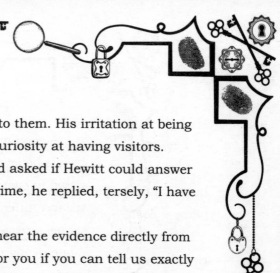

large moustache that joined on to them. His irritation at being disturbed was matched by his curiosity at having visitors. When Holmes introduced us and asked if Hewitt could answer a few questions regarding the crime, he replied, tersely, "I have already filed my report."

"Nevertheless, we'd like to hear the evidence directly from its source. There's a sovereign for you if you can tell us exactly what you saw and heard last night."

"I am a poor man," he said, as he gestured towards his surroundings, "but I am a proud one. You can keep your money. I'll happily help you catch the murderer and make the roads safer for all."

Holmes bowed, "We shall do our best."

Hewitt invited us into his home, which had only the barest of furnishings. There were no tables or chairs; the sole item of furniture was an upturned orange box. The whole room was none too clean. All the windows were boarded up. He lit a candle on a golden stick in the shape of Cupid who stood poised to shoot one of his arrows. The flickering light illuminated our surroundings only slightly. Nevertheless, the house was well built and the walls and doors, I could tell, were thick and sturdy. A dog howled outside, setting off a chorus of yips and barks. Hewitt put on a long shirt and rubbed his eyes.

"Blasted animals!" he said. "A man needs to get his sleep. I wish the landlord would take greater interest in this place and get rid of them. And they're an occupational hazard for a postman."

"I see," sympathised Holmes. "Thank you for agreeing to tell us about your discoveries."

"Happy to," said Hewitt. "How is the governess?

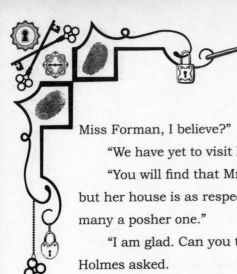

Miss Forman, I believe?"

"We have yet to visit her at Mrs Kemp's house."

"You will find that Mrs Kemp has simple tastes, as I have, but her house is as respectable as – perhaps even more so than – many a posher one."

"I am glad. Can you tell us about your round yesterday?" Holmes asked.

"It began much like any other. I picked up my mail and started shortly after noon. The rains had made it a difficult journey for the horses, and I was soaked from head to toe, but it was nothing we haven't braved before. I have driven along this road for many a year now."

"When did you first notice something was amiss?"

"I can't see very far ahead of my eye. Right where you are standing" – he pointed at me – "is as far as I can see since I lost my spectacles a few days ago. So the horses saw the carriage in front before I did, and we almost crashed. I got out to to calm the horses, then heard the gunshot. Or rather, my horses and I heard it, and we were frightened. It is not unusual to come across foxes in our path, but never have we heard a gunshot before. I can't say how long it took me to get the horses moving again. Ten minutes?

"At length we began to inch forwards and I came across the sorry sight. I got out of my carriage again and inspected the scene. Miss Forman was locked in the carriage and the coachman killed. I know my locks and that one was easy to pick. I am no doctor, but he was certainly dead and there was no helping the man. She, I could help, and sure enough, I did."

"What was the coachman's position when you found him?"

"He was slumped forward on his seat. At first I thought

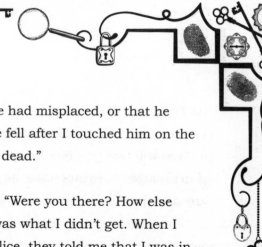

he was looking for something he had misplaced, or that he was drunk. It was only when he fell after I touched him on the shoulder that I realised he was dead."

"He was dry, wasn't he?"

Hewitt gave a violent start. "Were you there? How else would you have known? That was what I didn't get. When I raised the question with the police, they told me that I was in shock. I suppose I was, but my observations were not impaired. I was soaked to the bones, but the coachman was relatively dry."

Before Holmes could answer, there was a rattle on the door. Hewitt opened the door – much quicker than he had to Holmes and I – and a small street urchin appeared.

"I have messages for Mr Sherlock Holmes," the small boy squealed. Recognising my friend, he ignored Hewitt completely, bowed to Holmes and delivered two telegrams.

"The Baker Street Irregulars," Holmes said proudly to Hewitt, "are even more efficient than the telegraph service! Well done, Wiggins!"

Holmes tore open the envelopes and read their contents quickly. He withdrew a pencil and a slip of paper from his coat and wrote, with his firm hand, two short messages. I glanced over his shoulder as he was writing the second, which made no sense:

arrest bookworm street taxi*

What does the second message say?

Holmes turned and entrusted both messages to the boy.

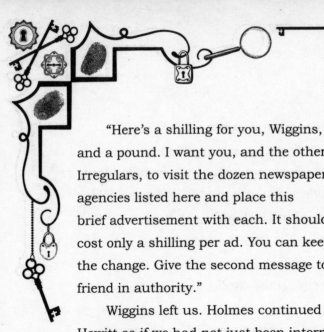

How much money will Wiggins get to keep?

"Here's a shilling for you, Wiggins, and a pound. I want you, and the other Irregulars, to visit the dozen newspaper agencies listed here and place this brief advertisement with each. It should cost only a shilling per ad. You can keep the change. Give the second message to our friend in authority."

Wiggins left us. Holmes continued his interrogation of Hewitt as if we had not just been interrupted and he offered no explanation.

"Did you search the coachman?"

"No."

"Did you come across a weapon?"

"No. Whoever killed the coachman must have taken it with him – or her. I couldn't see well. I could see little between his coat and the rain. I couldn't tell you where he was shot. I never saw the wound."

"Tell us about Miss Forman."

"I found her locked in the carriage."

"Was the door locked from the inside or the outside?"

"From the inside. She was lying prostrate in the car and, as I said before, the lock was not difficult to pick." He turned the ring on his finger as he spoke.

"It's an admirable skill to have! And were her clothes wet or dry?"

"Wetter than the coachman's, but not as soaked as mine."

"Did you find anything else in the carriage?"

"Yes, there was a copy of *Treasure Island*."

"Was it open or closed?"

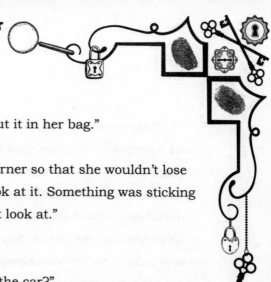

"Open, but I closed it and put it in her bag."

"Did you note the page?"

"No, but I bent the page's corner so that she wouldn't lose her place in the book. I didn't look at it. Something was sticking out of the pages that I also didn't look at."

"Did you look in her bag?"

"It's not my place, sir."

"Was there anything else in the car?"

"No."

"According to your report, you removed Miss Forman to your carriage and Mullins's corpse into hers."

"Yes. I had hoped to preserve the evidence as best I could. I also wanted to get some help for Miss Forman. Who knows when the next person would have come by? I took her with me. I hope that was the right thing to do."

"Your actions were faultless. In your place, I could not have done more. But one final question: did you drag or carry Miss Forman and Mullins?"

"I carried them both. I worried that I'd efface useful evidence otherwise."

"You'd make a model policeman. Very well done, sir."

At this, Hewitt positively beamed. Holmes gave him the sovereign and we took our leave. As we walked out of Hewitt's house, I noted that it was nice of him to give Wiggins and his crew an extra nine shillings, but then my curiosity got the best of me and I asked about the second message he had written.

"The message was coded with instructions for our friend Gregson," said Holmes. "I trust that he will be able to figure out the simple anagram, which tells him to meet us at Baker Street tomorrow at six."

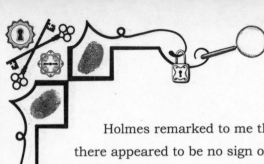

Holmes remarked to me that according to Hewitt's account, there appeared to be no sign of the children in the carriage. He wondered aloud where the children could be and whether he had missed something during our investigation so far.

"Did you notice, Watson, that when Hewitt spoke of picking the lock on Miss Forman's carriage, he fidgeted with his ring? This led me to notice two things. The first thing was the symbol on the ring. I've seen it before, but I cannot place it. The second was the bruising around it."

"Perhaps you're mistaken, Holmes?" I said, knowing full well that this would only encourage him to think harder.

Holmes also made note to ask Miss Forman about the copy of *Treasure Island*.

Out on the street, paperboys were plying their wares to passers-by. Holmes bought a *Daily Telegraph*, which he quickly skimmed before directing my attention to a short paragraph at the bottom of a page:

MUSEUM TRAGEDY CONTINUES

A second tragedy has befallen the Natural History Museum. This afternoon, Mr Charles Wright, 58, the recent victim of the museum break-in, died of a stroke. There is no susspicion of foul play. Wright was a security guard at the museum. Yesterday, he was struck on the head from behind. As reported, nothing was stolen from the mineralogy coollection, where Wright's round took him. No new information has surfaced.

At the tiime of death, Wright was at home and in the company of his wife. Mrss Wright reported that her husband has been unduly anxious in recent days. This is doubtless occasioned by the unfortunate incident at the museum. Wright will be soorely missed at the museum, where he made his rounds for the past four decades.

He has been unniformly described as a warm and friendly guard.

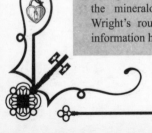

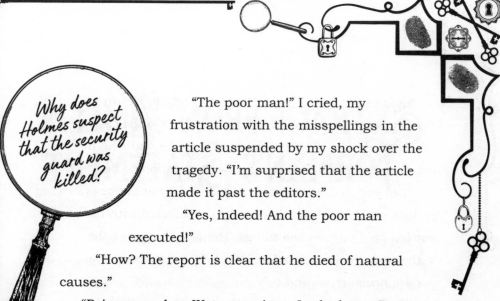

Why does Holmes suspect that the security guard was killed?

"The poor man!" I cried, my frustration with the misspellings in the article suspended by my shock over the tragedy. "I'm surprised that the article made it past the editors."

"Yes, indeed! And the poor man executed!"

"How? The report is clear that he died of natural causes."

"Poison, my dear Watson, poison. Look closer. Someone with influence is sending a coded message through the article. Wright's death is certainly connected to the burglary. I am surprised, though, how quickly it came. We will draw a net around his murderer soon."

Holmes can be the most trying of companions. His cryptic remarks are matched only by his subsequent reticence. From our brief acquaintance, though, I forbore pressing him for answers. I know that he will enlighten me further when the time is ripe. Still, his rather cryptic remarks piqued my curiosity.

If you are yet to visit Lord Bracewell, turn to page 16.

If you have visited Lord Bracewell, turn to page 37.

EXTRACT FROM AMELIA FORMAN'S STATEMENT

Thus far, I have pieced together the story from my recollections – with the occasional nudge from Holmes, who is far more forthcoming with criticism than with praise – and from sources such as telegrams, newspapers and diaries. The time is ripe, however, to hand over this narrative entirely to a different storyteller and it will imminently become apparent why.

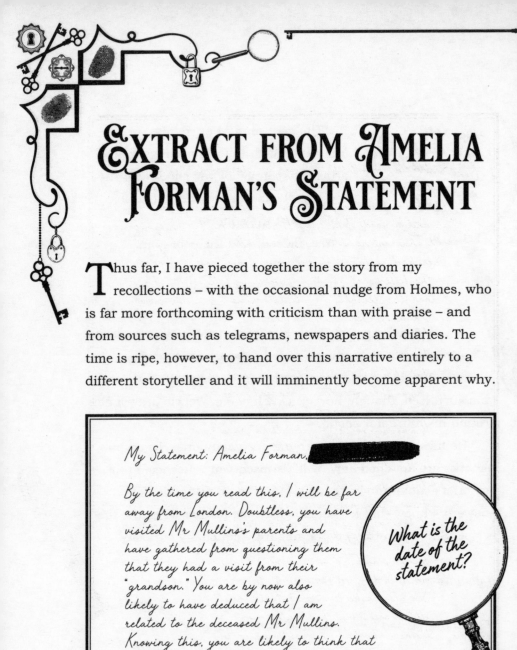

My Statement: Amelia Forman, ▬▬▬▬▬▬

By the time you read this, I will be far away from London. Doubtless, you have visited Mr Mullins's parents and have gathered from questioning them that they had a visit from their "grandson." You are by now also likely to have deduced that I am related to the deceased Mr Mullins. Knowing this, you are likely to think that my being on the carriage where he was found dead was no mere coincidence. However, I promise you that this was the work of chance. It is true that he left my mother in dire circumstances, and all my life I had always wondered about him.

What is the date of the statement?

When I was little, I made up stories about my real father, although I never shared these with anyone. Make no mistake: my mother's husband was a good man and a good stepfather. He treated me like his own child and continued to do so even after he and my mother had children of their own. I am close to Anne and the little ones as if they were my full sisters. I mourned the death of my stepfather as I would my own father had he been a decent man.

Nevertheless, I was curious about my true father. Was he like Long John Silver? Or Jean Valjean? Mindful of my mother's feelings, I never asked her about him. Then one day, I chanced upon her diary and came across a surname: Mullins.

It was not so very difficult to trace him once I had a name. Eventually, after her husband died, mother decided it was time for me to learn more about my father. While she did tell me a few stories of happy days they had spent together, she struggled to conceal her anger at the time he spent in the pub, his money troubles and his eventual desertion. I have a good memory and I pieced together the stories she told me.

She also spoke to me about his family on multiple occasions, specifically my grandfather, who had been wounded in the Crimean War. One day I stumbled across an article about a soldier who fitted the age he would have been at the time.

Mother pulled me aside one evening and gave me a locket that contained a

Where else have you heard about a similar item?

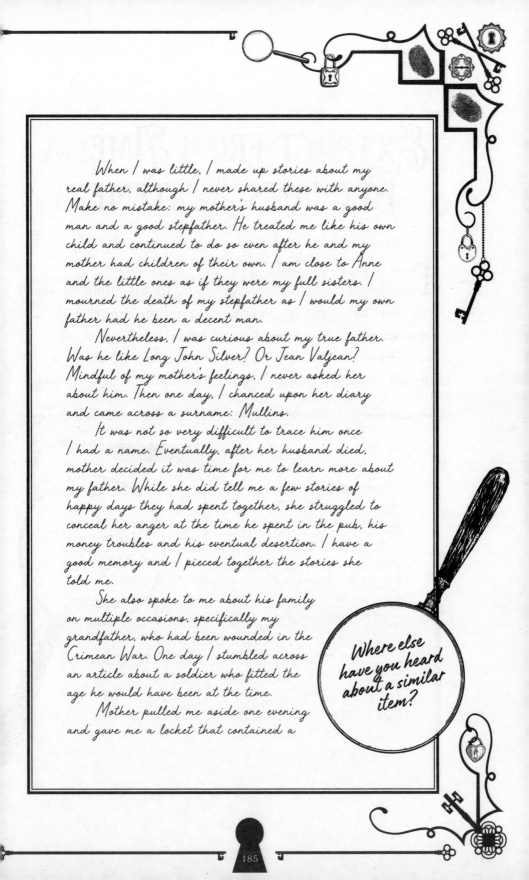

photograph of my real father. It also contained some strange symbols. She explained that this locket was the mirror image of one he had that contained her photograph, and the strange symbols were mirror images of my birth date. They were very much in love at that point in their lives, but something happened, and Harry Mullins didn't return to my mother - perhaps despite assurances that he would be back soon.

After seeing this, I needed to know why he left us. About a month ago, I traced my grandparents to Canterbury. I decided to visit them disguised as a young man, in case they did not know that their son had fathered a child. If they were as dismissive as their son appears to have been, I would not want there to be a traceable link between us, or for them to recognise me should they see me again.

Fortunately, they were the kind grandparents I had imagined over the years. When I showed them the locket and revealed that I was their grandchild, they offered to help me financially, with what little they could. They also told me about the character of their son... perhaps as a warning to prevent me from becoming involved with his schemes. What kind of a man would treat me, my mother and his parents as he did? He seems to have strung everyone along.

I asked for his address, but they refused to give it to me. I had come this far and hadn't expected to encounter this hurdle! I became enraged and stormed out of their house. I hadn't even revealed that they had a granddaughter instead of a grandson.

Once I arrived home, I thought some more about

why they would do such a thing. After calming down a little, I believed that they were trying to protect me. I decided against continuing my investigations into Harry Mullins, for what good could it possibly do to introduce myself to such a man?

With the past firmly behind me, I sought out a working situation via Cromwell's. They quickly found me a position, and a very good one at that. As chance would have it, I was to meet my father after all. I had learned from one of the photographs in my grandparents' house that Harry had a friendship with Lord Bracewell. I had not known who Lord Bracewell was until my grandparents mentioned that a generous lord in Finchley had helped him out of a few situations. It was only when Cromwell's provided me with the name of my new family and the location of the house that I realised the link.

Given this opportunity, I decided that I would confront Harry Mullins, but I would keep our connection a secret – even from him. I had planned to observe him from a distance while working at the estate, to learn more about him and to discover if he was the person described to me. Then, on the first day of my employment, I found myself his passenger: you cannot know how that felt! I was not prepared to meet him that quickly. I stole a glance at him when I boarded the carriage, but his cap and collar concealed most of his face and he said not a word to myself or the children.

I can tell you a little more about the murder and I hope that it will help you with your investigations

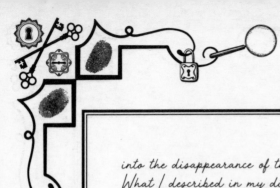

into the disappearance of the children, Mr Holmes. What I described in my diary was more or less correct: our carriage stopped, we heard a gunshot, then a loud thud on the carriage followed by moments of silence. I eventually disembarked in an effort to discover what had happened. I reached the front of the carriage and saw the driver depositing a body dressed like himself in the driver's seat. I had startled him.

"Get back in the carriage!" he ordered sternly as he turned to me. "And pretend that you saw and heard nothing." The wind blew strongly and pushed the cap and collar back from his face. This man standing on the carriage was not my father!

"Please do not harm the children or me," I begged. "We have done no wrong." The wind and rain were attacking us and I could barely keep on my own hat.

"No, but he has done plenty," said the mysterious man, looking at the body. "Mullins angered people who ought not be angered, and his reckoning has finally come. This will serve as notice to others who double-cross the powerful...".

I could not catch his every word. He might have said 'Moran,' 'Martin' or 'Malarkey'. He continued:

"Mullins should have heeded his warnings... as should you."

There was nothing I could do for the dead man, whatever our familial connection, but I could, however, try to protect my charges.

"What will become of us?" I asked.

"I mean you no harm. I have not been instructed to do anything else," he said. "Get back in the carriage.

Forget everything that you have seen and tell no one.
If he catches word of this conversation, I promise that
neither of us will live to see another day."

The inflection of the word 'he' and the fear in his
voice sent chills down my spine. I looked around us
but, from what little I could see, we seemed quite alone.

"How would anyone know of this conversation?"
I risked another question, my eyes darting back
and forth.

"He knows all and can read us through and
through. He may well be watching us even now. If he
meets you, he will see in your eyes, without you having
to say a word, that you know what happened here. Get
back in the car before it is too late, foolish woman!"
With that, he hopped off the carriage, but slipped at
the last moment and his hand fell against the side
panel, making a long scratch with his signet ring. He
recovered his footing and ran towards the grass and
into the trees, leaving me with the children and a dead
man. Or so I thought.

This time, I went to obey him, but when I opened
the carriage door, the children and their dog had
disappeared. I had forgotten to lock them in during my
haste to leave the carriage. Thinking that they wouldn't
have gone far, and I would see them hiding in the trees
soon enough, the opportunity to look upon the face of my
father was too great. I climbed into the driver's seat
and pulled up his hat. His face was frozen in anger
and fear, yet some of his features were as familiar to
me as my own reflection. I recoiled in shock and fell
from the driver's seat, hitting my head on the ground.

The rest of my story is as I told it in my diary. I briefly came to, crawled to the carriage and locked myself inside. I woke up the next morning at Mrs Kemp's house and have been here ever since. I was brought here by Mr Hewitt, the postman, and he has been so kind as to pay me a visit since then.

I am now leaving Mrs Kemp's. I know that the police will never believe my story, even if you might, and there is nothing I can do to change that.

I am sorry to have lost the children while they were in my care. I do hope that you find them soon, and safe. I regret that I cannot help you find them. Please do make amends to Mrs Kemp if you are able. She has been an ideal hostess and I have exploited her hospitality. If the words the mysterious man spoke are true, I may have already caught the attention of the mysterious 'Moran', 'Martin' or 'Malarkey', and will spend my life looking over my shoulder. No doubt the man who can effortlessly read minds will haunt my dreams. I shall not be returning home, for fear of bringing danger to my family. I wish that we had met under more amiable circumstances and I hope for our paths to cross again.

Amelia Forman

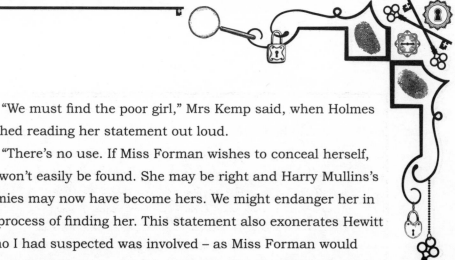

"We must find the poor girl," Mrs Kemp said, when Holmes finished reading her statement out loud.

"There's no use. If Miss Forman wishes to conceal herself, she won't easily be found. She may be right and Harry Mullins's enemies may now have become hers. We might endanger her in the process of finding her. This statement also exonerates Hewitt – who I had suspected was involved – as Miss Forman would have realised if the mysterious man was Hewitt. My apologies, my dear lady," he said to Mrs Kemp.

"Then what next?" I asked. "Do we find Mullins's killer?"

"I will certainly look into it, but with caution. I can, however, offer Mrs Kemp some comfort: I know who occupied your empty flat."

"Who?" Mrs Kemp and I asked at the same time.

"Mullins, of course. You see, I am convinced that Mullins rented the flat so that he could secure the money he was hiding

away from those he owed. He had no connection to Mrs Kemp, so there would be no reason for them to look here, especially as it is a boarding house for women. As a handyman, it would be an easy feat for him to install a secret door in the room, so that he could come and go unobserved. We are not far from the taverns he frequented, so he could easily take the money he cheated from people and hide it back here on the premise of stepping outside to smoke a cigar – most probably the type that we found at the crime scene."

"All of our links are broken," I told Holmes, in something bordering despair. "Miss Forman was our final hope of finding the children."

"No, I have known where the children are all along. They made it clear in their copy of *Treasure Island.* They spelled out 'Help' on the map. Where else have we seen a map that the children would know? They inadvertently left a small clue to their location."

Where are the children?

"You mean they were never kidnapped?" exclaimed Mrs Kemp.

"Never. When Miss Forman left the door of the carriage open, Spot must have jumped out – as dogs will – and ran away. The children will have followed him. They are familiar with this area, having grown up here. But running away from the man they loved as a second father – remember they believed Mullins to be driving the carriage – as well as their new governess, is likely to have resulted in a scolding. Where else would they go other than home? It is not far from here.

"They have concealed themselves in the cave on the estate,

the one that Mr Welsh, the pub's landlord, mentioned. This is where he played so many years ago. No doubt the children mean for their father to recover them: he has become a stranger for far too long and they desire his attention, understandably. If you fancy some exercise, I say we bring them home for supper."

As the door to Mrs Kemp's establishment closed behind us, I pondered a single question, which I articulated to my companion: "Holmes, why did you leave the children missing for all this time, only recovering them now?"

"My reasons are twofold. First, I knew that the children were safe and possibly comfortable in the cave. I surmised that they would have rations with them, as they are used to slipping in and out of the house undetected. And if they were to become troubled, they could find their way home easily enough."

How did Holmes know that the children had ample rations?

"But Holmes," I asked. "How did you know that the children were not starving or in want of anything?"

As a reply, Holmes reached into his pocket and pulled out a crushed purple wildflower. I remembered from our walk through the estate that they grew in one patch to the east. Holmes had found this flower on the stairs that had led down to the children's nursery. I looked at him in amazement.

"You shouldn't sleep so deeply, Watson," Holmes said. "The night we spent at Westwood Manor allowed me to investigate the recent renovations to the house. While I was having coffee in the dining hall the next morning – before you awoke – I discovered where the cave was located on the estate. I found the cave, met the children and heard their side of the story. They stubbornly

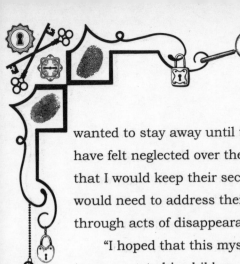

wanted to stay away until their father came for them. They have felt neglected over the past few months. I assured them that I would keep their secret for a while longer, but that they would need to address their father directly in future, rather than through acts of disappearance.

"I hoped that this mystery would pressure Lord Bracewell to open up to his children. He has become unduly selfish. Now, with no mother, no governess and with Mullins gone, it behoves Bracewell to spend more time with them."

"Will we meet Miss Forman again?" I asked.

"Who can say?" Holmes replied. He whistled as he strolled down the stairs and it was all I could do to keep up with him.

We went back to Westwood Manor. Holmes asked me to stand in the dining room and observe its decorations. After ten minutes or so of looking at the various Bracewell portraits, and using my rubbing of the estate map, I was able to determine where the cave was located.

Where is the cave in which the children are hiding?

I talked with Lord Philip Bracewell as we walked across the estate to the cave, and commented on his ingenious way of hiding the directions to the cave in plain sight.

"I've always wanted the children to learn more about the family history," he said. "What better reminder of the path to the secret cave than the portraits of their forefathers? The oldest portrait in the dining room is my great-grandfather, who hangs in the south of the room; my grandfather's portrait is on the east side; my father's is to the north, under the stained-

glass window depicting the north star, and then my own portrait is to the west. Using the house as the starting point, going south along the estate map, then east, then north and then west, we shall find the cave and my children in the forest glen.

"I promise you, Mr Holmes," Lord Bracewell said with conviction, "I shall be a more attentive father to them, and I shall ensure that Harry Mullins's parents are taken care of. If Miss Forman ever returns, I shall endeavour to help her as well."

We found the children, and their dog, and left them in Lord Bracewell's care.

"Our business here is concluded," said Holmes. "But our work is not yet complete. There is another mystery that requires our attention. We must not forget the Natural History Museum break-in. For that, we must return to Baker Street to meet Gregson."

Now turn to page 204.

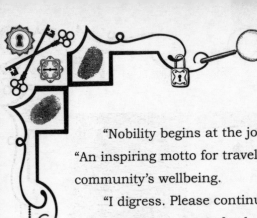

"Nobility begins at the journey's end," mused Holmes. "An inspiring motto for travellers who are responsible for a community's wellbeing.

"I digress. Please continue your story."

"The old man was fond of poker and he lost a fortune here one night. Father ran this establishment back then. He kept a chest for Edward, custom-made to his exact design specifications by one of the local woodworkers, for storing money to fund his games. It's still over in the corner, bolted to the wall and floor, if you want to see it. Only Edward knew the combination. It has been locked for at least four decades. Let me fetch us more coffee and check on my other patrons."

When Welsh left us Holmes and I strolled over to the large wooden chest.

"I wonder if it is truly empty," I said.

"There is only one way to find out," Holmes replied, as he ran his fingers over the intricate design on the top.

The chest lid was painted with five playing cards comprised of the jack of clubs, the two of spades, the six of clubs, the seven of diamonds and the king of hearts, in two rows. On the top left of the painting, beside the jack of clubs, were two painted hearts, about the same size as those on the king. On the top right, beside the two of spades, was painted a single spade. On the lower left, beside the six of clubs, were three small clubs. Lastly, beside the king of hearts, were four small diamonds.

On the front of the chest, five wooden slats secured the lid to the chest itself. Each slat had numbers ranging from nought to nine. The first slat on the far left had one small dot on the end of the slat, the second had two dots, the third three dots, and so on through to the fifth slat.

"Obviously we must move the numbered slats in and out to create the number that will unlock the chest," said Holmes. "By my calculations, there are 100,000 possible combinations for a five-digit number with digits ranging from nought to nine. Too many for a random guess, so there must be something that hints at the correct combination."

Holmes studied the chest for a few minutes and tried a few combinations using the slats. "It is not the number on each card," he said. "That would be too easy, not to mention that the jack and the king cannot be represented by the digits nought to nine.

"Do you know how they would be represented in this fashion?" he asked.

"Why, of course Holmes," I scoffed; I am no stranger to card games. "The jack is eleven and the king thirteen, leaving the queen at twelve if you arrange the cards in order from low to high. An ace can be either one or thirteen,

Why can't the jack and king be represented by the digits nought to nine?

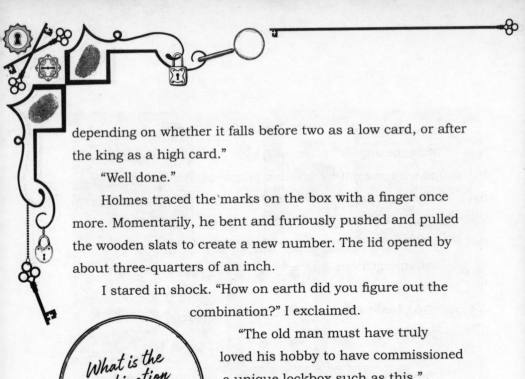

depending on whether it falls before two as a low card, or after the king as a high card."

"Well done."

Holmes traced the marks on the box with a finger once more. Momentarily, he bent and furiously pushed and pulled the wooden slats to create a new number. The lid opened by about three-quarters of an inch.

I stared in shock. "How on earth did you figure out the combination?" I exclaimed.

What is the combination that opens the chest?

"The old man must have truly loved his hobby to have commissioned a unique lockbox such as this," said Holmes. "As I mentioned, the combination is not based on the numbers depicted on the cards because the jack and king would not have numerical equivalents. Naturally, I selected the other thing found on each card in a standard deck."

"The suits?" I ventured.

"Exactly," said Holmes. "You must use both the number and the suit to figure out the puzzle. If you look at the painting of the cards, what else do you see?"

"There are smaller suits painted next to the cards. But what they represent, I do not understand."

"All in good time, Watson. This is to indicate that a spade has a single point at its tip, a heart has two rounded lobes at its top, a club has three rounded lobes and a diamond has four hardened points. Therefore, if you take the number of points and lobes in the order of the painted cards, you get...?"

"Three, one, four, four, two," I replied.

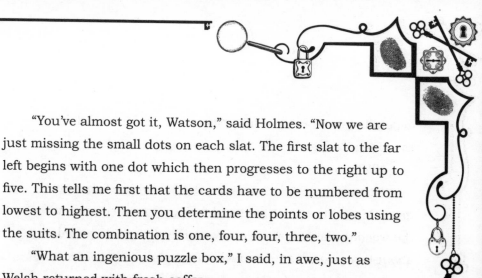

"You've almost got it, Watson," said Holmes. "Now we are just missing the small dots on each slat. The first slat to the far left begins with one dot which then progresses to the right up to five. This tells me first that the cards have to be numbered from lowest to highest. Then you determine the points or lobes using the suits. The combination is one, four, four, three, two."

"What an ingenious puzzle box," I said, in awe, just as Welsh returned with fresh coffee.

"By God," said Welsh. "You've opened the old box! Is there anything inside?"

"Some bills and a few receipts," Lestrade replied, as he leafed through the papers.

"That makes sense. Money was all Edward cared about." Holmes and I turned to Mr Welsh as he continued.

"He was an evil man and he would whip us children liberally. To this day I still have scars from some imagined wrongdoings. Cecil and I used to hide in our secret cave on the estate whenever he drank, as it was far away from the house.

"One night, drunker than usual, he whipped his horse savagely and was recompensed with a smart kick in the head. He never walked again but that only made him more bitter than ever. It was a relief for all concerned when he died a year later.

"Cecil was almost eighteen at that point and he spent most of his life in Australia, where he made his fortune. He returned to England with his wife and adult son, the present Lord Bracewell, Philip, who was nineteen before he even saw his ancestral home. With his monies, he made improvements to his neglected estate and restored to the family name some of its former glory. Philip Bracewell himself continued his father's good works. He is a clever fella and a hard worker. Any man

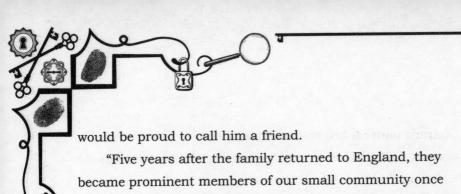

would be proud to call him a friend.

"Five years after the family returned to England, they became prominent members of our small community once more. Bracewell met his lady, herself an heiress of a substantial fortune, and he wooed her for two years before marrying her after another year's engagement. As I said, there never was a couple as deeply in love as 'em. The children followed two years after that and for a while they were all happy.

"Ever since her death, he has withdrawn from the public eye – I have seen him but once or twice – though he gives generously to many causes. When this house needed a new roof, he gave me the money without a second thought.

"If you go yonder, say a good word to Bracewell from me. He is a good'un, if distant, and aged before his time."

How old is the current Lord Bracewell?

"Such a sad story for a man so young," I said. "Only thirty-eight years old. We shall surely pass along your regards."

When the pub's proprietor had left, Holmes said: "There are, as far as I can see, three mysteries – three that may or may not be connected," he surmised as he knitted his brows and stroked his chin. "There is the case of the coachman, who was murdered prior to the abduction. What do we know of him?"

"Mullins had been working for the Bracewells for almost five years," said Lestrade. "According to the locals, he was eminently reliable. A professional detective, like myself, pursues all lines of inquiry."

"How many locals did you interview?"

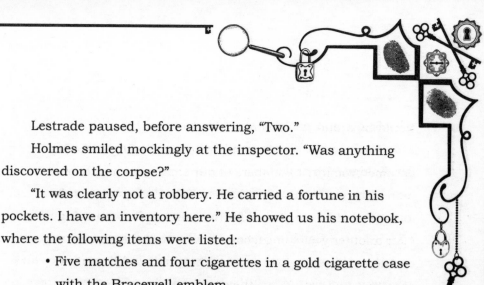

Lestrade paused, before answering, "Two."

Holmes smiled mockingly at the inspector. "Was anything discovered on the corpse?"

"It was clearly not a robbery. He carried a fortune in his pockets. I have an inventory here." He showed us his notebook, where the following items were listed:

- Five matches and four cigarettes in a gold cigarette case with the Bracewell emblem
- Four sovereigns and £20 in notes
- A locket containing a picture of his fiancée
- A note containing strange symbols, signed by 'M'
- A gold ring
- A few sugar cubes wrapped up in a handkerchief

"We await the verdict of the coroner's jury, which may take a few days, but it seems clear that he died of a gun wound, fired from no great distance."

"Miss Forman's narrative invites other kinds of questions: what was happening outside the carriage when it stopped? Had she spoken to Mr Mullins before his death? Had she seen the abductors prior to their being kidnapped? The diary stopped before she could report any of this. We are assuming that both Miss Forman and her diary are entirely reliable.

"Finally, where are the children?" Holmes asked.

"Surely the three mysteries – the coachman's death, what was happening outside the carriage and where the children are – are connected," Lestrade said.

Holmes shook his head slowly: "One ought not to make assumptions of that kind until we have more concrete evidence. What we have are the consequences and not the causes. If the mysteries are linked, then why did the assailant or assailants

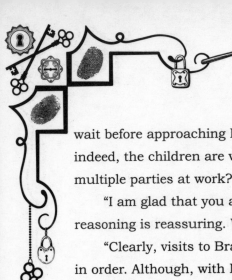

wait before approaching Miss Forman and the children – if, indeed, the children are what the criminals are after? Are there multiple parties at work?"

"I am glad that you are here, Mr Holmes. Your calm reasoning is reassuring. What is your plan?" Lestrade asked.

"Clearly, visits to Bracewell, Hewitt and Miss Forman are in order. Although, with Miss Forman still indisposed, we can postpone our visit to her. Have you got the addresses of the postman and Mrs Kemp?"

"Certainly," Lestrade replied. He jotted them down in his notebook, tore off the page and handed it to Holmes.

"Come now, Watson, we shall see if we can shed some light on this unfortunate business before the sun sets." We left Lestrade and the pub. The fresh air, cold and wet as it was, did me the world of good. I felt invigorated and I could tell it had a similar effecton my companion.

"Whom shall we visit first?" I asked Holmes.

If you think Holmes and Watson should visit Lord Bracewell first, turn to page 175.

If you think Holmes and Watson should visit Hewitt the postman first, turn to page 36.

"Eternal nobility belongs to those upon whom it is conferred?" I asked.

"No," said Holmes. "That can't be it. Nobility cannot be eternal, much as nobles may wish it. Inherited? Yes, but noble families die out and they fall in and out of favour with each reigning monarch."

Now turn to page 106.

A DIAMOND IN THE ROUGH

When Holmes and I returned to our rooms at 221B Baker Street, we found Inspector Tobias Gregson of Scotland Yard in the study reading the evening paper.

"I have followed your directions, Mr Holmes." Gregson showed Holmes the message that Mrs Hudson had left on the door. "I understand that you have been trying to keep our meetings out of the public eye so did not want us to be seen together for more than a few moments. I admit it took me some time to decipher your puzzle, but I did so successfully!" He saw my confounded expression and handed me the message. It read:

Dear Gregson,

Watson and I have been unavoidably detained. As you were unable to figure out my simple anagram, I'm hoping you can redeem yourself with this one.

Look above your head and you will find 10 metal keys hanging from the soffit:

1 black key with a circular head   1 silver key with a circular head

1 black key with a triangular head   1 silver key with a triangular head

1 black key with a square head   1 silver key with a square head

1 black key with a pentagonal head   1 silver key with a pentagonal head

1 black key with a hexagonal head   1 silver key with a hexagonal head

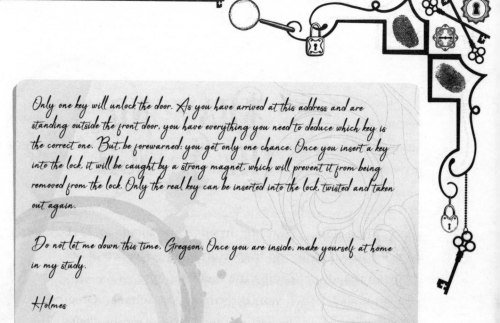

Only one key will unlock the door. As you have arrived at this address and are standing outside the front door, you have everything you need to deduce which key is the correct one. But, be forewarned: you get only one chance. Once you insert a key into the lock, it will be caught by a strong magnet, which will prevent it from being removed from the lock. Only the real key can be inserted into the lock, twisted and taken out again.

Do not let me down this time, Gregson. Once you are inside, make yourself at home in my study.

Holmes

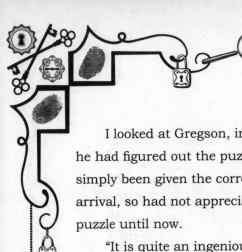

I looked at Gregson, impressed that he had figured out the puzzle. I had simply been given the correct key upon arrival, so had not appreciated this puzzle until now.

Which key opens the lock to 221B Baker Street?

"It is quite an ingenious lock system, Holmes," exclaimed Gregson. "When I arrived at Baker Street, I found the ten keys hanging above the door. As your only instructions were that 'I have everything I need because I have arrived at this address,' I made the assumption that the key had something to do with the address itself – 221B Baker Street. The digits of 221, when added together, give the number five, which correlated to the pentagonal key heads. The 'B' told me it was the black key rather than the silver. The door opened easily. I stepped inside, replaced the key and made myself at home. You have quite a collection of interesting, and odd, things. Now, why have you sent for me? Your message gave no explanation."

"All in good time, Gregson," said Holmes. "With a pinch of luck, we will get to the bottom of the Natural History Museum business tonight. You will shortly hear the full details of an interesting case. Could you be so kind as to add another log to the fire and fetch some coffee from the kitchen, while Watson and I remove our coats and discuss our next steps?"

Gregson soon returned to the study with a tray of coffee.

As we warmed ourselves with our beverages, Holmes began his tale: "The puzzle of the museum is simple once we isolate the facts. You recall that the glass shards were cleared away. This could have been to cover up someone breaking into the museum – or breaking out of it. But the thief made a grave mistake here, which I will explain presently.

"When Mr Wright, the security guard, was knocked unconscious, a case of theft became one of assault. Now that he has passed away, it has escalated to manslaughter or even murder."

What does Holmes infer from the Telegraph article about Mr Wright's injury?

"Mr Wright must have been involved in the crime," said Holmes. "He was struck on the head from behind. The attacker would have drawn attention to himself after breaking the window, so he couldn't have approached the security guard without him noticing. It follows that Mr Wright felt comfortable turning his back on whoever was in that room with him – most likely an accomplice.

"Let us continue: the article says nothing appears to have been stolen. And it appears true that nothing was removed. But was an item in the mineralogy collection replaced with something else? Something that would not look out of place?

"If that were the case, why this particular exhibit? It must appear inconspicuous in its new surroundings: a stone or jewel, surely, like so many others in the exhibit. I will go further. The mysterious circumstances of the break-in distracted the authorities, but an item in a public exhibition is likely to have been seen by experts on numerous occasions and would be widely recognised. My hypothesis is that the stone that was switched belongs to a private owner."

"If that is the case, why has the owner not come forward?" Gregson asked. "Wouldn't the owner of something that valuable check that their property was safe once they heard about the break in?"

"A good question, Gregson. My theory is that the museum officials believe nothing was stolen; a message they will have passed to owners of private exhibits. They claim that 'everything was accounted for,' which can be read as *nothing was stolen*," Holmes stressed this last phrase. "My other suspicion is that the private owner of the stolen gem might have a dubious claim to it, so is keen to avoid a formal investigation from Scotland Yard."

Holmes changed tack. "What clues do we have from the crime scene? The lack of muddy footprints may suggest that the culprit concealed himself within the museum after closing time, attacked the guard and escaped through the window. Alternatively, the culprit may not have left the crime scene at all. Aside from the broken glass, there is no evidence that anyone journeyed through that window. However, there were curious scratches on the museum floor. Would the guards not have heard the sound of breaking glass had someone been trying to get in?

"Merton and Wright were the two museum security guards at the scene. They had access to the crime scene during their day jobs and were able to revisit it – along with the other collections in the museum – without attracting suspicion. They were ideally positioned to switch an item at their convenience. None of these circumstances, of course, implicates them."

"One moment, Holmes!" I interrupted, "I follow your reasoning, but how would they go about finding a suitable facsimile that would stand the scrutiny of an initial examination, especially by experts in the field?"

Where did the guards get a replica gem to take the place of the stolen one?

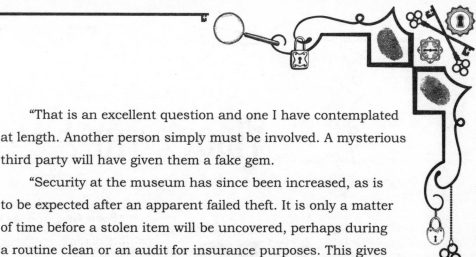

"That is an excellent question and one I have contemplated at length. Another person simply must be involved. A mysterious third party will have given them a fake gem.

"Security at the museum has since been increased, as is to be expected after an apparent failed theft. It is only a matter of time before a stolen item will be uncovered, perhaps during a routine clean or an audit for insurance purposes. This gives the thief – or thieves – a brief opportunity to get rid of the gem – especially if they are avoiding the gem's owner as well as the authorities.

"If the previous owner's claim to the gem is disputable, then they may resort to drastic measures to recover the jewel, and it follows that they would begin their enquiries with those at the crime scene. Our mysterious third party, the supplier of the fake gem and the true thief, will remain hidden from the owner and can therefore escape the crime without repercussion. The mastermind behind this has created scapegoats in the security guards – red herrings for the owner to chase.

Gregson and I exchanged a look. This was all starting to fall into place. But who was behind it all?

"It would be folly to surmise further without tests. So, I dispatched two telegrams along my messenger network, the Baker Street Irregulars. I know a little something about the seven or eight leading jewel thieves in London and its surrounds. After they posted my advert in the newspapers, my request to Wiggins was for the Irregulars to keep a lookout for these thieves. And I was rewarded for my efforts: the whereabouts of two of the thieves has been unknown for the past two days.

"If you recall, Watson, I sent a telegram from here on

Sunday morning after we received the telegram from Lestrade asking us to meet him in Finchley. The telegram I sent before we departed was to Sir Anthony Borrs, curator of the mineralogy collection, and husband of a former client. I wrote to him to say that I have a priceless jewel that I would like to sell and asked where I might list it. I deceived Borrs, you see, because I could not be absolutely sure that he was not involved in the crime. I then planned to pose not as a seller, but as a buyer who would attract the attention of a thief planning to get rid of a gem recently acquired.

"I advertised in all of the places Sir Anthony mentioned, and received a favourable response from one James Monday, requesting a meeting at seven this evening. My last message was to you, Gregson," said Holmes. "I wanted you here by six o'clock this evening so we could have this very conversation and prepare to close the case."

The doorbell interrupted Holmes, who glanced at the clock on our mantelpiece. It read 6.30 p.m.

"Our visitor, I see, is early – likely to throw us off guard. Gregson, can you ready your handcuffs? Watson, kindly stand by the door and prevent his or her escape."

Holmes went downstairs to answer the door. A few minutes passed. I heard Holmes ask a young man to remove his boots, as one was scratching Mrs Hudson's newly cleaned floors. The man argued for a few moments, but eventually relented, and came upstairs with his boots in one hand, which struck me as unusual. Holmes led him into the study where Gregson and I were waiting anxiously.

The man understood the situation at once but was too slow to get away. I had blocked the door and Gregson was upon him instantly. He put up a struggle, dropping his boots in the process. Holmes picked them up, set them aside and helped Gregson and me subdue him. It was all the three of us could do to keep him in check. In seconds, it was over. He was handcuffed and sat between Gregson and me. He glared angrily at the three of us in turn.

"What have you jumped me for?" he shouted. "I am here to sell a piece of jewellery. There's no crime in that."

"None whatsoever, Mr Monday – if that is truly your name," said Holmes. "Except that what you have to sell does not belong to you." He dangled the man's boots in front of him.

What does Holmes suspect about the mysterious Mr Monday?

"It is best if you answer us honestly," said Holmes gently. "Mr Monday, or, if I may address you by your real name, Mr Merton."

The man's shoulders slumped.

"How did you know?" he asked quietly.

Holmes turned over one of the boots. Shards were embedded in the bottom of the boot. They twinkled in the light from the fire. "Your boots were scratching my floor when you entered the house. It was at that point that I knew for certain that Mr Miles Merton, the guard on duty at the Natural History Museum during an attempted theft last Saturday, had just walked in. The same scratches were found on the floor beneath the window at the museum. It is also apparent that you were complicit in the theft, which was set up under the guise of attempted theft.

"My name is Sherlock Holmes, and these are my associates, Dr John Watson and Inspector Gregson of Scotland Yard.

Perhaps it's best if you tell us your story."

"I will be honest when I say that I do not know everything," he said.

"Let us be the judge of that," said Holmes.

Merton sighed. "Near the end of my watch a few weeks ago, Charlie – Mr Wright – tells me that he had been made an attractive offer: he was promised £10,000 if he could swap a real gemstone in the museum with something that looked close enough to be the real thing. Wright would need my help because we share a watch. I also believe that he did not fully trust his accomplice, but Charlie would reveal nothing more about him... perhaps because he didn't know any more himself. I know Charlie to be a thoroughly good, dependable bloke and I agreed to a ten per cent cut."

"You had planned to make the transaction at the museum, but it was interrupted," prodded Holmes.

"Charlie's partner didn't trust us, you see, so he insisted on being in the museum at the time," said Merton. "Just before closing, we hid him in an alcove near our patrol route. He brought the fake stone with him and handed that to Charlie while I stood guard. Charlie had just picked the lock on the case and made the switch when we heard another guard doing his rounds further down the corridor. This startled Charlie's accomplice, so he ran back into the alcove out of sight. With all the patrols inside and outside the building, we had to make a commotion to help him escape. Charlie yelled and the accomplice looked towards the hallway to see if the other guards were coming.

"Charlie tossed me the stone while the accomplice wasn't looking, closed the case and then – to the annoyance of his accomplice who stood hidden nearby – smashed the nearest window.

"I put the stone in my boot and as I turned around saw poor Charlie clubbed in the head by the accomplice, who then leaned down to search him – probably to take the stone. I shouted again, as the other security guards were on their way, and the man jumped through the window and ran off. I stepped through the window to see if I could see which way he went. That must have been when I stepped in the glass.

"Then I ran over to Charlie, who was unconscious. The other guards arrived to help, so I stepped back. By that time, we were all looking around to see if anything had been taken. I cleaned up the glass while the building and grounds were searched. When the police questioned me, I told them that we saw a man hiding in the hallway and that I shouted after he injured Charlie."

"Can you describe the man?" asked Gregson.

"He was a short and round man, with a reedy voice. He had a full beard that covered most of his face."

"I believe the beard to be a fake," said Holmes. "That man has been trying to track our movements to find the stone since we left here on Sunday morning. Little did he know, we were working on another case, rather than investigating the museum break-in. Carry on."

Where have you come across this man before?

"There's not much more to say," said Merton. "With Charlie first in hospital unconscious, and now dead, I don't have any way of contacting his accomplice. Not that I would want to after what he did to my friend."

"Once he failed to deliver the gem, it is likely that the mysterious, bearded man contacted his own boss – the person who wants the gem – to pin the theft on you and save his own skin," said Holmes. "And you are now looking to get rid of the stone. You and Mr Wright – Charlie – were the only two people identified at the scene of the crime. You know that the person who orchestrated the theft will pursue you to the ends of the earth for the gem, as will the owner of the stone."

"You are not of this world, sir! How did you read my mind?" Merton asked, surprised for the first time this evening. "After Charlie's death, I couldn't sleep a wink. I planned to sell the gem as soon as possible and leave the country. Charlie's accomplice knew that I was involved, but he didn't know that I had the gem. Although I knew that he would figure that out fairly soon."

"The bearded man has either escaped or is dead – or he soon will be. Of that, I am sure," said Holmes. "It looks like he has upset a powerful and influential man. That may be his boss, or it may be the owner of the stone. Whoever it is, they insinuated through a newspaper article that your friend, Mr Wright, was poisoned due to his involvement in the theft. You are a clever man, so you know your friend's death was not accidental."

"I had my suspicions when he suddenly took a turn for the worse," said Merton. "I visited his wife Sunday morning who gave me a roughly sketched map that had been found in his jacket. It led me to a hiding place inside the museum. In the bottom of a planter he had hidden the £10,000."

He looked remorseful as he said: "I was foolish to get involved with any of this."

"But wisely, you did not visit the hospital," I said.

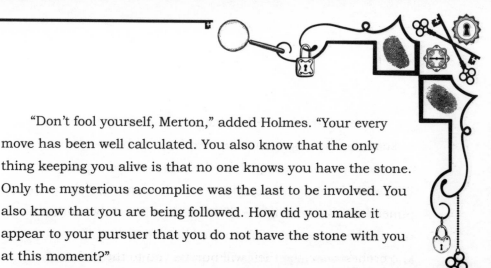

"Don't fool yourself, Merton," added Holmes. "Your every move has been well calculated. You also know that the only thing keeping you alive is that no one knows you have the stone. Only the mysterious accomplice was the last to be involved. You also know that you are being followed. How did you make it appear to your pursuer that you do not have the stone with you at this moment?"

"I went for a swim at the local baths," said Merton. "I secured the stone behind a broken tile as soon as I entered the changing room, then put all of my belongings in my locker. After my swim I saw that my locker had been broken into and my possessions searched. The place was empty by that point, so I grabbed the stone again and made my way here. Now that I have thrown them off my scent, they will look elsewhere. But I dare not return home. I will take the money that Charlie hid away and leave England."

"You are a wise man, indeed. But you must have been curious about the jewel's worth, since that would determine the efforts they would go to find you? Have you garnered that information from the museum?"

Merton nodded. He cocked his head and motioned towards his pocket, from which I removed a small envelope. I passed it to Holmes, who opened it and looked at the paper inside.

"This is certainly enough for a man to kill for... even multiple times," murmured Holmes. "The diamond is worth almost £80,000!"

Holmes looked at Merton. He turned Merton's left boot upside down, and a large diamond tumbled into his hand. He threw the stone to an astonished Gregson and placed the boots on the floor in front of Merton.

"And now it's time to release you, Merton. I expect you will remain alive as long as you never return. I believe that you are as safe as you can reasonably expect to be in your position. The weighted chain of worry you wear is more than adequate punishment for your mistake. Gregson will make sure that the stone is returned to the collection with little fanfare. If it looks like it was never stolen, then no crime has seemingly been committed and neither the owner, the thief nor the authorities will have any need to pursue you."

We released Merton, who pulled on his boots and headed to the door. Just before he left the room, he turned to Holmes and said, "Thank you, Mr Holmes. You have been good to me. I have one point – perhaps a discovery – to divulge. The fake jewel was kept in a box inscribed with an 'M'."

At this mention, Holmes and I stared at each other in shock.

Where have you seen the letter 'M' before?

"You are sure it was an 'M'?" asked Holmes. "There were no other markings on this case? Where is the box now?"

"I am sure, Mr Holmes," said Merton, who was anxious to leave. "The bearded man took it with him. I, for certain, do not want to cross him."

"It is too bad," said Holmes. "It might have been able to tell us more about 'M'."

Merton did not reply. He left our study and we could hear him walking down the stairs. Gregson left shortly thereafter.

"Imagine that," I said. "This mysterious 'M' is now connected to this crime as well as to the recent departure of Mr Harry Mullins. Do you think that the reason Mullins died was

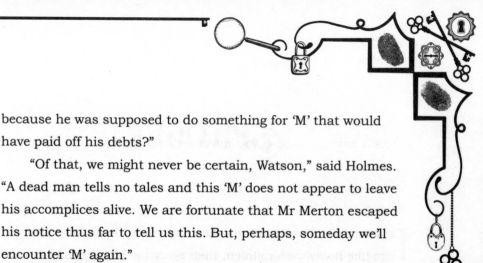

because he was supposed to do something for 'M' that would have paid off his debts?"

"Of that, we might never be certain, Watson," said Holmes. "A dead man tells no tales and this 'M' does not appear to leave his accomplices alive. We are fortunate that Mr Merton escaped his notice thus far to tell us this. But, perhaps, someday we'll encounter 'M' again."

I wrote an 'M' in my notebook, circled it and put a large question mark after it. I shuddered to think of the influence and power this man had in order to pull off such crimes, especially without detection. A demand from Holmes brought me out of my dark thoughts and into the present.

"Now, let us think of lighter things, Watson," said Holmes. "If you will pass me my Stradivarius, I shall play you songs without words by one of my favourite composers."

I passed Holmes his violin and he began to play.

The setting sun cast long shadows across the floor, and the flickering firelight made the wooden furniture glow. The mysterious notes on the violin filled the study as Holmes became lost in the music. I sat back in the chair, closed my eyes and listened to Mendelssohn's songs without words, or *Lieder ohne Worte*. It had been a long few days and I would soon have to start my write-up of our most recent adventure.

But first, I must finish writing what I am calling *The Sign of the Four* and think of a title for another recently solved mystery containing a ghostly hound. There is much for me to do!

Now turn to page 218.

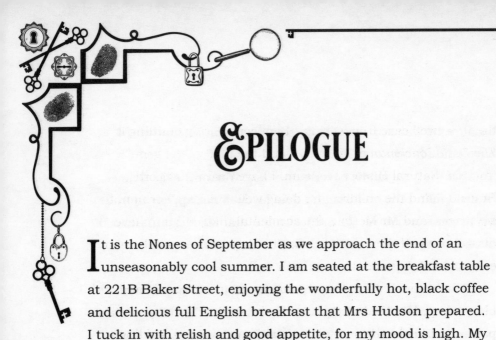

EPILOGUE

It is the Nones of September as we approach the end of an unseasonably cool summer. I am seated at the breakfast table at 221B Baker Street, enjoying the wonderfully hot, black coffee and delicious full English breakfast that Mrs Hudson prepared. I tuck in with relish and good appetite, for my mood is high. My new mystery series, *The Sign of the Four*, has gained popularity among the masses over the last few months, and the final instalment is to be published at the end of this week.

The publisher is already asking me about the next series and feels that the otherworldly subject matter of my next venture will give us our best success to date. I have a number of our smaller cases to write up first, after which I shall have time to provide the proper attention to, as I am calling it, *The Hound of the Baskervilles*. Holmes still seems indifferent to my publishing our adventures, yet he cannot deny that the fame they have brought him allows him to pick and choose the cases that most take his fancy.

What is today's date?

Holmes was up early this morning. He has already breakfasted and is sitting in his favourite armchair reading the morning paper.

I am resolved to start outlining my story on the Baskerville family, but my thoughts have been disrupted as I think back to

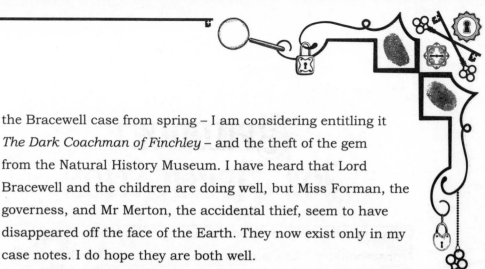

the Bracewell case from spring – I am considering entitling it *The Dark Coachman of Finchley* – and the theft of the gem from the Natural History Museum. I have heard that Lord Bracewell and the children are doing well, but Miss Forman, the governess, and Mr Merton, the accidental thief, seem to have disappeared off the face of the Earth. They now exist only in my case notes. I do hope they are both well.

A light touch on the arm shook me from my reverie and, as I looked up, Mrs Hudson pointed to the study. From my vantage point, I could see the side of the chair, and Sherlock holding his pipe and the corner of a newspaper. I looked at Mrs Hudson quizzically. She put a finger to her lips and motioned for me to move closer.

I slid around the table to get a better look at the study. To my astonishment, sitting in his lap on top of the morning paper was the first part of our series published in the pennies: *A Study in Scarlet*. And, even more astonishingly, sitting atop the detective's head was the deerstalker cap.

"A deal is a deal, Watson," intoned Holmes.

Dr John Watson

Appendix 1: Job Application

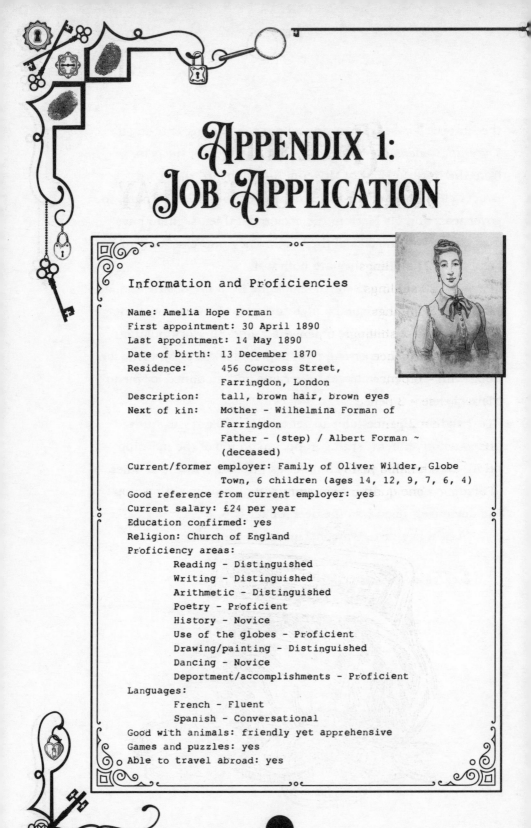

Information and Proficiencies

Name: Amelia Hope Forman
First appointment: 30 April 1890
Last appointment: 14 May 1890
Date of birth: 13 December 1870
Residence: 456 Cowcross Street,
                 Farringdon, London
Description: tall, brown hair, brown eyes
Next of kin: Mother - Wilhelmina Forman of
                 Farringdon
                 Father - (step) / Albert Forman ~
                 (deceased)
Current/former employer: Family of Oliver Wilder, Globe
                 Town, 6 children (ages 14, 12, 9, 7, 6, 4)
Good reference from current employer: yes
Current salary: £24 per year
Education confirmed: yes
Religion: Church of England
Proficiency areas:
        Reading - Distinguished
        Writing - Distinguished
        Arithmetic - Distinguished
        Poetry - Proficient
        History - Novice
        Use of the globes - Proficient
        Drawing/painting - Distinguished
        Dancing - Novice
        Deportment/accomplishments - Proficient
Languages:
        French - Fluent
        Spanish - Conversational
Good with animals: friendly yet apprehensive
Games and puzzles: yes
Able to travel abroad: yes

APPENDIX 2: CURRENCY OF THE DAY

Guinea = 21 shillings

Pound = 20 shillings

Crown = 5 shillings

Half-crown = 2 shillings, 6 pence

Shilling = 12 pence

Sixpence = 6 pence

Threepence = 3 pence

Tuppence = 2 pence

Penny

Halfpence = half a penny

Farthing = one quarter of a penny

Appendix 3: Chess set

1 king   1 queen   2 bishops   2 knights   2 rooks   8 pawns

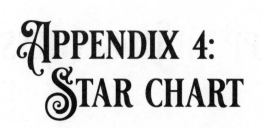

APPENDIX 4: STAR CHART

12 DECEMBER 1881

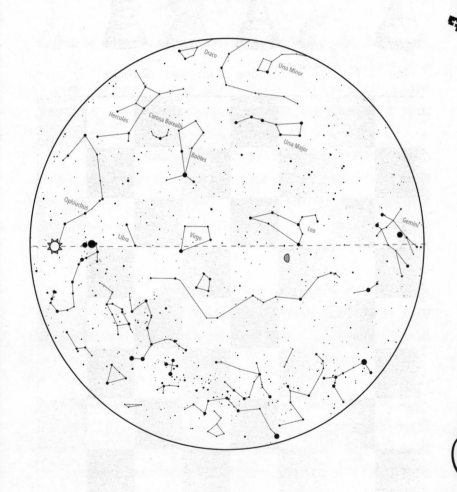

HINTS

Page 34: Why was Holmes suspicious?

What did Holmes and Watson see multiple times prior to leaving the train?

Page 109: Why was Holmes reviewing the diary so closely and what did he discover?

Hint 1: What can you infer from the "neat and precise" writing?

Hint 2: What do you think he could smell?

Page 7: What year does the story take place?

Hint 1: How does the knowledge of "the Jefferson Hope affair" help you determine the date?

Hint 2: Jefferson Hope is referenced in *A Study in Scarlet*, which has just been published.

Page 14: What is the answer to the riddle?

Hint 1: What shrinks as time passes?

Hint 2: What object's "life" provides clarity as it is used, slowly fading into dark?

Page 50: For what two reason did the undercook blush and leave the room?

Hint 1: What was she being teased about?

Hint 2: What was wrong with the breakfast she prepared for Mullins?

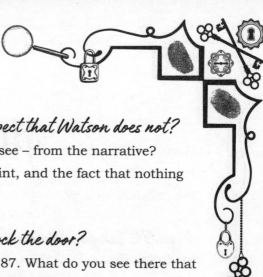

Page 11: What does Holmes suspect that Watson does not?

Hint 1: What do you see – or not see – from the narrative?

Hint 2: What does the previous hint, and the fact that nothing was stolen, tell you?

Page 108: How did Holmes unlock the door?

Hint 1: Refer back to pages 86 to 87. What do you see there that may match something in the illustration?

Hint 2: Something was "three-quarters full" and in the colour of moonlight.

Page 34: Where in town are they to meet Lestrade?

Hint 1: Refer to the telegram again. Who wears a crown, and where is a crown worn?

Hint 2: Where would you meet for a drink?

Page 197: Why can't the jack and king be represented by the digits nought to nine?

If the ace is low, what numbers are the jack and the king? What numbers are they if the ace is high?

Page 114: Where is Amelia's treasured diary hidden? How do you know?

What usually "marks the spot" in *Treasure Island*?

Page 104: How long has Lestrade kept the crime out of the papers?

Take another look at the newspaper article and Amelia's last diary entry. When did those events occur? What part of the day is it today?

Page 86: What drink are they supposed to order?

Hint 1: What are these ingredients?

Hint 2: What drink is known for its association with a fairy in the colour of spring?

Page 111: Can you translate the exchange between Amelia and Miss Stoper?

Answer: "Are you competent enough to teach small children?"

"Of course, Madam! I speak French very well. The last family I worked for often spent their summers in Paris, so the children had daily lessons. My father is French."

Page 98: What is Miss Stoper's motivation for setting up the theft?

She complained to Holmes and Watson earlier about this.

Page 112: What is Amelia's annual salary?

Hint 1: Count the letters in the name of each month and see which number corresponds with where the month falls in the year – that is the correct month.

Hint 2: How many Kings named Henry were there? How many are in a baker's dozen?

Page 102: Where did Lestrade find Amelia's diary?

Where else have you seen something that might look like the tips of arrows?

Page 32: How does Watson get them out of the carriage?

Find the item hidden in the illustration that would help you to open a door.

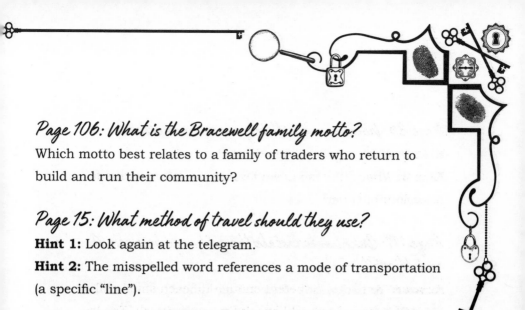

Page 106: What is the Bracewell family motto?

Which motto best relates to a family of traders who return to build and run their community?

Page 15: What method of travel should they use?

Hint 1: Look again at the telegram.

Hint 2: The misspelled word references a mode of transportation (a specific "line").

Page 183: Why does Holmes suspect that the security guard was killed?

Hint 1: What does Watson note?

Hint 2: Note the extra letters. What do they spell?

Page 198: What is the combination that opens the chest?

Hint 1: Use the smaller suits on the corners of the painting to determine the number of points/lobes for each suit. Three small clubs painted beside the six of diamonds indicates three lobes, for example.

Hint 2: Each slat has a dot, or a series of horizontal dots, on it. That tells you to order the cards from lowest to highest.

Hint 3: Use the lobes (points) on each suit to work out the code.

Page 13: Where are Holmes and Watson to meet Lestrade?

Look at the first letter of each new line, after "STOP".

Page 88: What is the typical annual salary for a governess at this time?

Hint 1: The Queen here is Queen Victoria.

Hint 2: Dumas' novel is *The Three Musketeers*.

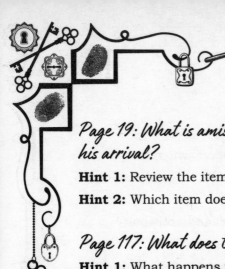

Page 19: What is amiss that Holmes has detected since his arrival?

Hint 1: Review the items from the Bracewells' travels.

Hint 2: Which item doesn't fit in?

Page 117: What does the code say?

Hint 1: What happens to the message if you shift each letter forwards or backwards along the alphabet?

Hint 2: Try moving each letter four spaces.

Page 39: How does Holmes escape the locked room?

Hint 1: A copy of *Jane Eyre* is needed for this puzzle. If you do not have a copy, you can visit Project Gutenberg online.

Hint 2: The column header 'C' stands for 'Chapter'.

Hint 3: CPSW = Chapter Paragraph Sentence Word. Find the words to reveal a message.

Page 200: How old is the current Lord Bracewell?

Use all references to Lord Bracewell and his family.

Page 17: What road should they take to get to the main gate of Westwood Manor?

Review Watson's map on page 101 to find the shortest route.

Page 94: How did Holmes deduce the combination?

Hint 1: The order is given in the text, if you know what to look for.

Hint 2: Note Miss Stoper's age and the beginning of the summer that she became employed. Remember, she changes the combination yearly.

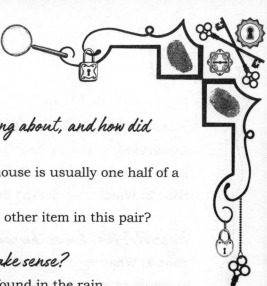

Page 65: What is Mrs Kemp lying about, and how did Holmes know?

Hint 1: One item in Mrs Kemp's house is usually one half of a pair. Which item?

Hint 2: Who do you think has the other item in this pair?

Page 27: Which item doesn't make sense?

Hint 1: Recall that the body was found in the rain.

Hint 2: Which item would not have survived the rain?

What is missing?

Hint 1: Recall the conversation with Lestrade about items found at the scene.

Hint 2: What would you expect to have been recovered from the scene?

What would Holmes have expected to be recovered from the scene?

Hint 1: What sound was heard when the carriage stopped?

Hint 2: How could this sound relate to the way Mullins died?

Page 179: What does the second message say?

Hint 1: This is an anagram.

Hint 2: The word next to the * appears in the solution.
Unscramble the rest of the words to form a phrase. There are five words in the solution.

Page 133: Which constellation is missing? Why did the Bracewells leave it out?

Why might this constellation be important to the Bracewells?

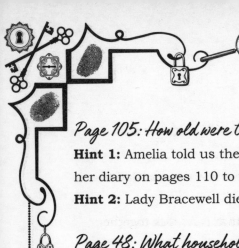

Page 105: How old were the children when their mother died?

Hint 1: Amelia told us their age – and that they were twins – in her diary on pages 110 to 116.

Hint 2: Lady Bracewell died five years ago.

Page 48: What household liquid should the maid not mix with the cleaning solution?

What should you never mix with vinegar when creating cleaning supplies?

Page 53: What did Holmes infer about the scratch?

What item, worn on the hand, could cause a dull, wide scratch?

Page 41: What is the answer to Holmes's puzzle?

Hint 1: This clock moves 90 minutes on its face for every 60 minutes of real time.

Hint 2: Write down two columns, each starting with 12 noon. One column is the broken clock; the other is the real time. When do they match again?

Page 176: What is George Hewitt's address?

Does it help to move the page?

Page 47: Can you match the chessboard to the story? Use the blank chessboard on page 222.

"Wall" refers to a Rook; "confessing" refers to a Bishop.

Page 66: What is it about Mrs Kemp's garden that links her to George Hewitt?

What do you see in the pattern of Mrs Kemp's garden layout?

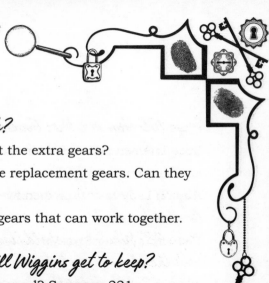

Page 45: Can you fix the clock?

Hint 1: What do you notice about the extra gears?

Hint 2: Look at the notches in the replacement gears. Can they be stacked?

Hint 3: There is only one pair of gears that can work together.

Page 180: How much money will Wiggins get to keep?

Hint 1: How many shillings in a pound? See page 221.

Hint 2: He has 21 shillings (1 pound + 1 shilling); 12 papers = 12 shillings.

Hint 3: The first shilling was for Wiggins, for delivering the messages. The pound (20 shillings) was for the Irregulars to post the adverts.

Page 128: Is there a pattern to the scratches in the table?

Hold the picture parallel to your eyes then slowly tilt the book away from you in two directions.

Page 55: What is it about this address that distracts Holmes?

Who will work in this building a few years later?

Page 184: What is the date of the statement?

Hint 1: When did the incident with the carriages take place?

Hint 2: How many days ago was that?

Page 58: How did Holmes unlock the box?

Hint 1: Who shoots their arrows through hearts?

Hint 2: Where else in the house did you see a "To my love" engraving? Whose partner was Psyche?

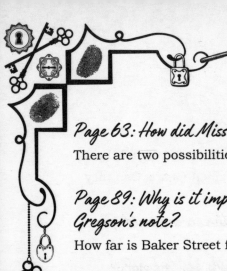

Page 63: How did Miss Forman escape from this room?

There are two possibilities for her escape.

Page 89: Why is it impossible that Holmes received Gregson's note?

How far is Baker Street from their current location?

Page 52: What did Holmes see at the crime scene that Watson did not?

Hint 1: Review the illustration of the crime scene on page 103.

Hint 2: Look more closely at the puddles.

Page 218: What is today's date?

Hint 1: When is the Nones of September?

Hint 2: What clues are in Watson's daydream?

Page 97: Why is Mr Cromwell unable to open the safe?

It was noted that Mr Cromwell had trouble holding onto his book. Even Holmes struggled to turn the dial.

Page 153: Who does Holmes suspect might have been involved with this crime?

Hint 1: Who was in the right place at the right time?

Hint 2: Things are not necessarily as they seem: who would you not expect to be a suspect?

Page 147: Can you judge this book by its cover?

Hint 1: Study the cover of the book and see if you can determine the answer to this part of the mystery.

Hint 2: Find the letters and unscramble the word.

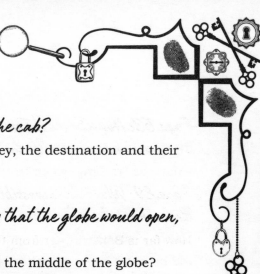

Page 70: Why did Holmes stop the cab?

Plot the starting point of the journey, the destination and their current location on a map.

Page 158: How did Holmes know that the globe would open, and how to open it?

Hint 1: What was running around the middle of the globe?
Hint 2: Where did Lord Bracewell grow up?

Page 119: What is the address of Mullins's parents' house?

Set up a pair of dice as is seen here. Then turn them towards you, in the direction of the arrow. What numbers appear?

Page 125: What do the symbols mean?

Hint 1: What happens if you place a mirror in the centre of each symbol?
Hint 2: Where have you seen this date before?

Page 149: Why does Holmes suspect that the person they met is not the real Lord Bracewell?

What can you deduce from the portrait of Lord Bracewell on page 20, and from the letter on page 37 he wrote to Holmes?

Page 185: Where else have you heard about a similar item?

Which item found on Mullins's body might be relevant here?

Page 67: What has Holmes deciphered about the mysterious note?

Hint 1: It cannot be read from left to right.
Hint 2: What can you use to read the image?

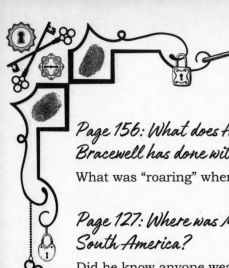

Page 156: What does Holmes suspect the imposter Lord Bracewell has done with the files?

What was "roaring" when they entered the room?

Page 127: Where was Mullins getting the money to move to South America?

Did he know anyone wealthy who could have helped him?

Page 161: What is the date of the statement?

Hint 1: When did the incident with the carriages take place?

Hint 2: How many days ago was that?

Page 79: What does Amelia now suspect?

Hint 1: What did the laundress reveal about Hewitt's connection to the Bracewell household?

Hint 2: Does Hewitt have a motive for a crime against Mullins?

Page 123: What has aroused Holmes's suspicions about Joshua's story?

When was the Crimean War?

Page 208: Where did the guards get a replica gem to take the place of the stolen one?

Would they have been able to carry out this crime on their own?

Page 61: What is unusual about this room?

Hint 1: Review the illustration. With the window painted shut, and a double-locked door, where could there be a point of entry or exit?

Hint 2: Look closely at the wall by the bookcase.

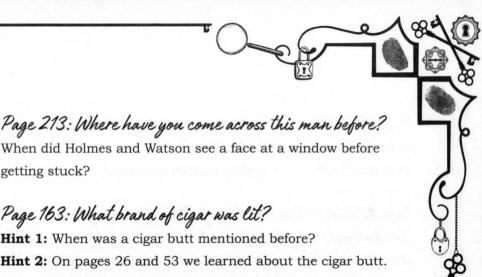

Page 213: Where have you come across this man before?

When did Holmes and Watson see a face at a window before getting stuck?

Page 163: What brand of cigar was lit?

Hint 1: When was a cigar butt mentioned before?
Hint 2: On pages 26 and 53 we learned about the cigar butt.

Page 165: Where did George Hewitt get the drugs from?

Hint 1: Where could he find medicinal plants?
Hint 2: Who in the story has a large garden?

Page 170: How did they stage the crime?

Hint 1: Review the crime scene illustration on page 103.
Hint 2: What would help them hoist a heavy body into a seat?

Page 167: Who does George Hewitt think can help them?

Hint 1: Who does he know that works in the house?
Hint 2: How might the staff of Westwood Manor be linked to Hewitt after generations of his family have worked on the estate?

Page 206: Which key opens the lock to 221B Baker Street?

Hint 1: What information did Gregson need to arrive at this door?
Hint 2: How can the address help you here?
Hint 3: Add together the digits in the address to determine the shape of the key.

Page 80: Where does Amelia suspect the children are?

What did she notice when she entered the house?

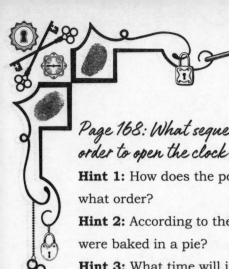

Page 168: What sequence of moves needs to be performed in order to open the clock door?

Hint 1: How does the poem relate to the clock, and in what order?

Hint 2: According to the nursery rhyme, how many blackbirds were baked in a pie?

Hint 3: What time will it be one hour later?

Page 146: Using the map and the note, find out what the children really had to say.

Hint 1: Using the map from *Treasure Island* on page 145 and the children's story, what can you see?

Hint 2: The course of their journey when charted on the map spells out a word.

Page 150: Can you answer the questions posed to Watson and Lestrade?

Whom has Bracewell lost recently?

Page 75: How did Amelia get the policeman to tell her about the crime?

If you were in her shoes, who would you tell him you were with?

Page 174: What is the hidden message in the letter from Lord Edward Bracewell?

Look at the first letter of each line.

Page 157: What could Watson identify about the shreds of paper?

What did he notice about the papers in Miss Stoper's safe?

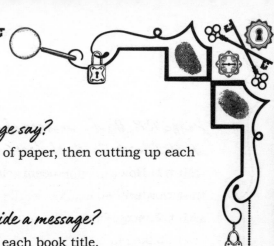

Page 82: What does the message say?

Try tracing the note onto a piece of paper, then cutting up each square and reordering them.

Page 24: Does the bookshelf hide a message?

Hint 1: Look at the first letter of each book title.

Hint 2: Why might one of the books be upside down?

Page 129: What is the identity of Mullins's child?

Compare the family photographs to another photograph you have seen.

Page 72: What is the date of the statement?

Hint 1: On what date were Holmes and Watson brought in on the case? The kidnapping and discovery of Mullins's body happened the day before.

Hint 2: They spent Sunday night at Westwood Manor and had breakfast there the next morning, when they spoke with Mrs Clemens.

Hint 3: All the other interviews and events happened on the same day as this.

Page 194: Where is the cave in which the children are hiding?

Hint 1: Review the description of the portraits on page 20. Is there a pattern to the positions of the Bracewell portraits?

Hint 2: How could this pattern relate to map coordinates, and in what order?

Hint 3: Where might you use these coordinates? Where on the estate would it be logical to start?

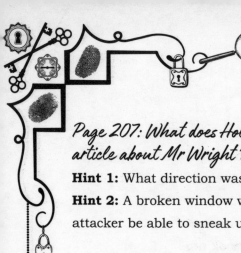

Page 207: What does Holmes infer from the Telegraph article about Mr Wright's injury?

Hint 1: What direction was Mr Wright struck from?

Hint 2: A broken window would surely make a noise. Would the attacker be able to sneak up on Mr Wright?

Page 192: Where are the children?

Hint 1: What might be a good hiding place on the estate, where their grandfather used to play?

Hint 2: Is there a spot on the map from *Treasure Island* that might have given them the idea?

Page 211: What does Holmes suspect about the mysterious Mr Monday?

Hint 1: Why did Holmes ask him to remove his boots?

Hint 2: How does this relate to the crime scene?

Page 216: Where have you seen the letter 'M' before?

What did the visitors to Mullins's parents tell them?

Page 69: Where in town are they to meet Lestrade?

Hint 1: Refer to the telegram again. Who wears a crown, and where is a crown worn?

Hint 2: Where would you meet for a drink?

Page 193: How did Holmes know that the children had ample rations?

What did Holmes find earlier in the story that proved the children had been in the house after their 'abduction'?

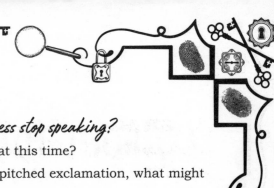

Page 78: Why did the laundress stop speaking?

Hint 1: How is Amelia dressed at this time?

Hint 2: If Amelia let out a high pitched exclamation, what might this have given away?

Page 29: What does the message from M say?

Can you decipher it using the grid below?

A B C   J K L
D E F   M N O
G H I   P Q R

S U   W Y
T V   X Z

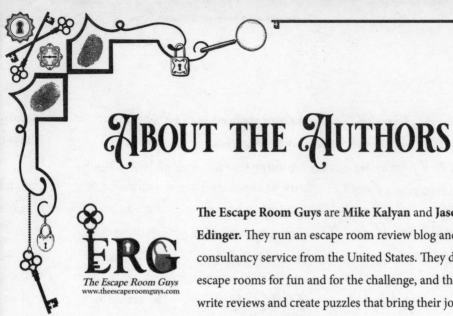

ABOUT THE AUTHORS

The Escape Room Guys are **Mike Kalyan** and **Jason Edinger.** They run an escape room review blog and consultancy service from the United States. They do escape rooms for fun and for the challenge, and they write reviews and create puzzles that bring their joy of escape rooms to others.
www.theescaperoomguys.com

The Escape Room Guys
www.theescaperoomguys.com

Tom Ue specialises in nineteenth-century British literature at Dalhousie University, Canada. He was editor of _Imagining Sherlock Holmes_, an issue of the _Journal of Popular Film & Television_. He has written extensively on Arthur Conan Doyle and his contemporaries, with his books including _Gissing, Shakespeare, and the Life of Writing_ (Edinburgh University Press) and _George Gissing_ (Liverpool University Press).

PICTURE CREDITS